Crime Passionnel

To Hugo, a young Party member, is assigned the job of working with a 'deviationist' Party leader as his secretary, and shooting him. This he does. . . . But did he camouflage a political assassination as a *crime passionnel*? The answer is made clear, when, on his release from prison two years later, he tries to explain to a former comrade, and to himself, just what his motives were.

In the words of *The Listener*, 'Jean-Paul Sartre is today the most discussed author in the world', and this is his most discussed play. First produced in Paris in 1948, it remains a classic analysis of the mentality and methods of Communism.

D0766415

The illustration on the front cover shows Michael Gough as Hugo in the production at the Lyric Theatre, Hammersmith. The photograph is reproduced by courtesy of Angus McBean. The photograph on the back cover is reproduced by courtesy of The Radio Times Hulton Picture Library.

CRIME PASSIONNEL

a play by

JEAN-PAUL SARTRE

translated by

KITTY BLACK

EYRE METHUEN LTD

11 NEW FETTER LANE, LONDON, EC4

First published in 1949
by Hamish Hamilton Ltd
First published in this edition 1961
by Methuen & Co Ltd

Reprinted 1965, 1969, 1973, 1978, 1980 and 1981
Reproduced and printed in Great Britain by
Whitstable Litho Ltd, Whitstable, Kent.

ISBN 0 413 31010 8

CRIME PASSIONNEL was presented at the Lyric Theatre, Hammersmith, on 16th June, 1948, with the following cast:

HOEDERER	Roger Livesey
HUGO	Michael Gough
JESSICA	Joyce Redman
GEORGES	Brian Carey
LEON	Julian Randall
SLICK	Max Brimmell
LOUIS	Raymond Westwell
CHARLES	Humphrey Heathcote
FRANZ	Gunnar Hafsten
OLGA	Yvonne Coulette
PRINCE PAUL	Ernest Clark
KARSKY	William Sherwood

The production was by Peter Glenville, and the décor by Rolf Gérard

On the 4th August, the play transferred to the Garrick Theatre.

Crime Passionnel

(*Les Mains Sales*)

CHARACTERS

HOEDERER, *one of the leaders of the Proletarian Party*

HUGO
JESSICA, *Hugo's wife*

GEORGES
LEON } *Hoederer's bodyguard*
SLICK

LOUIS
FRANZ
CHARLES } *Members of the Proletarian Party*
IVAN
OLGA

PRINCE PAUL, *son of the Regent of Illythia*
KARSKY, *secretary of the Pentagon Party*

The action of the play takes place in Illythia, an imaginary country in Central Europe.

Prologue

The scene is OLGA'S *flat. The ground floor of a maisonette, on the main street of a town. One feels that the person who lives in this room is quite indifferent to her surroundings. On the right are a door into the hall and a window with closed shutters. On the left, towards the back, another door and a fireplace with a mantelpiece and a mirror above it. At the back there is a telephone standing on a chest of drawers.*

Cars pass in the street from time to time. Traffic noises and motor-horns.

OLGA *is sitting in front of the wireless, fiddling with the controls. Static, then a fairly distinct voice.*

WIRELESS. German troops are retreating along the whole front. The Red Army has captured Kischner, forty miles from the Illythian frontier. Wherever possible, Illythian troops are refusing to engage; several detachments have already deserted to the Allies. Illythians, we know you were forced to take arms against the U.S.S.R., we know the deeply democratic feelings of the Illythian people, and we. . . .

OLGA *turns the knob. The voice stops. She remains motionless, her eyes fixed on space. Pause. Knock at the door. She starts. More knocking. She goes slowly to the door. More knocking.*

OLGA. Who is it ?
HUGO (*off*). Hugo.
OLGA. Who ?
HUGO (*off*). Hugo Barine.

OLGA *is visibly surprised, but continues to stand in front of the door.*

HUGO (*off*). Don't you know my voice? Open the door. (*She goes quickly to the chest of drawers, takes something out of a drawer with her left hand, wraps her hand in a scarf, goes to open the door, throwing it open and stepping back quickly to avoid surprise. A tall boy of 23 is standing in the doorway.*) It's me. (*They look at each other for a moment in silence.*) Are you surprised?

OLGA. You look so strange.

HUGO. Yes. I've changed. (*Pause.*) Well? Had a good look? (*Pointing to the revolver hidden under the scarf.*) You can put that thing away.

OLGA (*without putting the revolver down*). I thought you were given five years.

HUGO. That's right—five years.

OLGA. Come in and shut the door. How did you get out? (*She takes a step backward. The gun isn't actually pointing at* HUGO, *but very nearly.* HUGO *casts an amused look at it, then slowly turns his back on* OLGA *and shuts the door.*) Did you escape?

HUGO. Escape? I'm not crazy. They had to throw me out—by the seat of my pants. (*Pause.*) They released me for good conduct.

OLGA. Are you hungry?

HUGO. You'd like that, wouldn't you?

OLGA. Why?

HUGO. A man looks so harmless when he's eating. (*Pause.*) No, thank you—I'm neither hungry nor thirsty.

OLGA. Yes or no would have been enough.

HUGO. Don't you remember? I talk too much.

OLGA. I remember.

HUGO (*looking round him*). How bare it all looks, and yet everything is still the same. My typewriter?

OLGA. Sold.

HUGO. Oh? (*Pause. He looks round the room.*) It's empty.

OLGA. What's empty?

HUGO (*with an all-embracing gesture*). All this: the furniture looks as if it's floating in a vacuum. Back there, if I stretched out my arms, I could touch both walls of my cell. Come closer. (*She doesn't move.*) I had forgotten; out of prison, people live at a respectful distance. What a lot of waste space! It's funny to be free, makes you feel giddy. I'll have to get used to talking to people with the width of a room between us.

OLGA. When did they release you?

HUGO. Just now.

OLGA. You came straight here?

HUGO. Where else could I go?

OLGA. You haven't talked to anyone?

HUGO (*looks at her and starts to laugh*). No, I haven't. It's all right. (OLGA *relaxes a little and looks at him.*) Are you glad to see me?

OLGA. I don't know. (*A car passes. The horn sounds.* HUGO *shivers. The car drives past.* OLGA *watches him coldly.*) If you really have been released, you don't have to be afraid.

HUGO (*ironically*). Think so? (*He shrugs his shoulders. Pause.*) How's Louis?

OLGA. All right.

HUGO. And Laurent?

OLGA. He—he had bad luck.

HUGO. I thought so. I don't know why, I always thought of him as being dead. There must be plenty of changes?

OLGA. It's all much more difficult. The Germans are here.

HUGO (*indifferently*). Oh? Since when?

OLGA. Three months. Five divisions. They were supposed to be going through on their way to Hungary. But they just stayed.

HUGO. Oh? You must have quite a few new members?

OLGA. Yes. Recruiting isn't done in quite the old way. There are gaps to fill; we are . . . we have become less strict.

HUGO. Yes, of course; you've got to adapt yourselves. (*With slight anxiety*.) But, essentially, things are still the same?

OLGA (*embarrassed*). Well . . . broadly speaking, naturally.

HUGO. Anyway, you're still alive. It's difficult to realize, in prison, that other people go on living. Do you ever talk about me?

OLGA (*lying badly*). Sometimes.

HUGO. The boys come on their bicycles, at night, like we used to do. They sit round the table. Louis fills his pipe and someone says: it was a night like this that the kid volunteered for a special mission?

OLGA. Something like that.

HUGO. And then you say: he did a good job. He did it cleanly, without compromising anyone.

OLGA. Yes, yes, yes.

HUGO. Sometimes the rain used to wake me up. I used to say to myself: maybe tonight they'll be talking about me. It was my main advantage over the dead; I could still think you were thinking of me. (OLGA *takes his arm with an involuntary and awkward movement. They look at each other*. OLGA *drops his arm*. HUGO *stiffens a little*.) Then, one day, you said to each other: he's still got three years to go and when he comes out . . . (*Changing his tone without taking his eyes off* OLGA.) . . . and when he comes out, by way of reward, we'll shoot him down like a dog.

OLGA (*recoiling abruptly*). Are you crazy?

HUGO (*pause*). Did they make you send me the chocolates?

OLGA. What chocolates?

HUGO. Liqueur chocolates, in a pink box. For six months I used to get parcels regularly from someone called Reich. I didn't know anyone of that name, so I knew the parcels came from you and I was glad. They stopped coming, and I thought: they have forgotten me. Three months ago, a parcel arrived, from the same sender, with chocolates and cigarettes. I smoked the cigarettes, and my next-door neighbour ate the sweets. The poor chap was very ill. Very ill indeed. Then I knew you hadn't forgotten me after all.

OLGA. Hoederer had friends who couldn't have been very fond of you.

HUGO. They wouldn't have waited two years to let me know. No, Olga, I had plenty of time to think it all out, and I could only find one explanation. At first, the Party thought I might still be useful. Afterwards, they changed their minds.

OLGA (*without hardness*). You talk too much, Hugo. Far too much. You don't feel alive unless you're talking.

HUGO. I talk too much. I know too much, and you've never trusted me. That's all there is to it. (*Pause.*) I don't blame you, you know.

OLGA. Hugo, look at me. Do you really believe what you're saying? (*She looks at him.*) Yes, you do. (*Violently.*) Then why come here to me? Why, why?

HUGO. Because you would never be able to shoot me. (*He looks at the revolver she is still holding and smiles.*) At least, that's what I thought. (OLGA *angrily throws the revolver and scarf on the table.*) You see?

OLGA. Listen, Hugo, I don't believe a word of your story, and I've had no orders. But if ever I do, you'd better know that I would do as I was told. And if someone from the Party questioned me, I'd tell them you were here, even if I knew they'd shoot you down in front of me. Have you any money?

HUGO. No.

OLGA. I'll give you some. Then you must go.

HUGO. Where? Skulk in the side streets, or on the docks? The water is cold, Olga. No matter what happens, it is warm here, and there are lights. It would be more comfortable to end here.

OLGA. Hugo, I shall do as the Party orders. I swear I'll carry out their orders.

HUGO. You see it's true.

OLGA. Get out of here.

HUGO. No. (*Imitating* OLGA.) 'I'll carry out their orders.'

You've some surprises coming to you. With the best will in the world, what you do is never what the Party orders. 'Go to Hoederer and fire three shots into his stomach.' That's clear enough, isn't it? I went to Hoederer, and I fired three shots into his stomach. But it was all quite different. Orders —there were no orders. Up to a point, it's easy, then there are no more orders. The orders were left behind. I had to go on alone, I killed all alone and . . . and I don't even know why any more. I wish the Party would order you to shoot me. Just to see what would happen. Just to see.

OLGA. You'll see. (*Pause.*) What are you going to do now?

HUGO. I don't know. I hadn't thought. When they opened the prison gates I thought I'd come here, and I came.

OLGA. Where is Jessica?

HUGO. With her father. She wrote to me sometimes, in the beginning. I don't think she's using my name any more.

OLGA. What do you expect me to do with you? Some of the boys come here every day. They come and go as they please.

HUGO. Do they use your bedroom too?

OLGA. No.

HUGO. Then I'll go in there. There was a red coverlet on the divan, the wallpaper had a pattern of yellow and green diamonds. There were two photographs on the wall. One was of me.

OLGA. Taking an inventory?

HUGO. No, I'm remembering. I thought about it a lot. The second photo gave me something to worry about: I couldn't remember whose it was.

A car passes in the street. He starts. They are both silent. The car stops. A door slams. Someone knocks at the door.

OLGA. Who is it?

CHARLES (*off*). Charles.

HUGO (*in a whisper*). Who's Charles?

OLGA (*whispering*). One of us.

HUGO (*looking at her*). Well?

A very short pause. CHARLES *knocks again.*

OLGA. Well, what are you waiting for? Go into my room. You can check up on your souvenirs.

HUGO *goes out.* OLGA *opens the door.* CHARLES *and* FRANZ *are there.*

CHARLES. Where is he?

OLGA. Who?

CHARLES. You know. We've been trailing him since he left the jug. (*Brief silence.*) Isn't he here?

OLGA. Yes, he's here.

CHARLES. Where?

OLGA. In there. (*She points to her room.*)

CHARLES. Good.

He makes a sign to FRANZ *to follow him, puts his hand in his pocket and takes a step forward.* OLGA *bars his way.*

OLGA. No.

CHARLES. It won't be long, Olga. If you like, take a walk outside. When you get back, you won't find anyone, and no traces either. (*Meaning* FRANZ.) That's what he's here for.

OLGA. No.

CHARLES. Let me get on with the job, Olga.

OLGA. Did Louis send you?

CHARLES. Yes.

OLGA. Where is he?

CHARLES. In the car.

OLGA. Go and fetch him. (CHARLES *hesitates.*) I told you to go and fetch him.

CHARLES *makes a sign and* FRANZ *disappears.* OLGA *and* CHARLES *remain facing each other, in silence.* OLGA, *without taking her eyes off* CHARLES, *picks up the scarf wrapped round the revolver.* FRANZ *returns with* LOUIS.

LOUIS. What's the matter ? Why are you interfering ?

OLGA. You're in too much of a hurry.

LOUIS. Too much of a hurry ?

OLGA. Send them away.

LOUIS. Wait for me outside. If I call come back. (*The* MEN *go out.*) Well now, what do you want to say to me ?

OLGA (*gently*). Louis, he worked for us.

LOUIS. Don't be a baby, Olga. He's a dangerous type. He must be made to keep his mouth shut.

OLGA. He won't talk.

LOUIS. He's the bloodiest talker. . . .

OLGA. He won't talk.

LOUIS. I wonder if you really see him as he is. You've always had a crush on him.

OLGA. And you've always been against him. (*Pause.*) Louis, I didn't ask you to come here to discuss my feelings, I'm talking in the interests of the Party. We've lost so many people since the Germans came. We can't allow ourselves to lose this boy without even finding out if he's fit for salvage.

LOUIS. Fit for salvage ? He's an undisciplined little anarchist, an intellectual who thought of nothing but taking up attitudes, a bourgeois who worked when he felt like it, and dropped the whole thing for a yes or a no.

OLGA. And yet, when he was twenty, he killed Hoederer in the midst of his bodyguard, and camouflaged a political assassination as a *crime passionnel*.

LOUIS. Was it really a political assassination ? That's never been properly cleared up.

OLGA. Exactly; we ought to clear it up now.

LOUIS. The whole story stinks; I wouldn't touch it with a barge-pole. Anyway, I've no time to make him pass examinations.

OLGA. I have. (*Movement from* LOUIS.) Louis, I'm afraid you may be putting too much personal feeling into this affair.

LOUIS. I'm afraid you may be making the same mistake.

OLGA. Have you ever known me give way to my feelings? I don't ask you to let him live unconditionally. I don't give a damn for his life. All I say is that before you wipe him out we ought to find out if he can be re-admitted to the Party.

LOUIS. The Party could never admit him again. Not now. You know that as well as I do.

OLGA. He worked under an assumed name. No one besides ourselves knows him now. Are you afraid he'll talk too much? If he is properly looked after, he won't talk. You say he is an intellectual and an anarchist? Maybe, but he's a desperate man too. If he is properly used, he could become the mainspring of all sorts of jobs. He has proved it once.

LOUIS. What do you suggest?

OLGA. What's the time?

LOUIS. Nine o'clock.

OLGA. Come back at midnight. I'll find out why he shot Hoederer, and what sort of man he has become. If I think he can work with us again, I'll tell you through the door, you'll leave him alone tonight, and come back and give him his orders tomorrow.

LOUIS. And if he's not fit for salvage?

OLGA. I'll open the door.

LOUIS. A lot to risk for very little.

OLGA. Where's the risk? You've got men round the house?

LOUIS. Four.

OLGA. Keep them there. (LOUIS *doesn't move*.) Louis, he worked for us in the past. We must give him a chance.

LOUIS. All right. I'll be back at midnight.

He goes out. OLGA *goes to the bedroom door and opens it.* HUGO *comes out.*

HUGO. It was your sister.

OLGA. What?

HUGO. The other photo. It was your sister. (*Pause.*) You've taken mine down. (OLGA *doesn't reply. He looks at her.*)

You're looking rather strange. What did they want?

OLGA. They were looking for you.

HUGO. Oh. Did you tell them I was here?

OLGA. Yes.

HUGO. I see. (*He makes a move to go.*)

OLGA. It's a fine night and there are men round the house.

HUGO. Oh? (*He sits at the table.*) Give me something to eat.

> OLGA *fetches a plate, bread and ham. While she is arranging the plate and food in front of him he speaks.*

I was quite right about your room. I remembered everything. Everything was just as I remembered it. (*Pause.*) When I was in jail, I used to think: it's all a memory. Now the real room is there, on the other side of the wall. I've been into it. I looked at your room and it didn't seem any more real than it did in my memory. The cell too, that was all a dream. And Hoederer's eyes, the day I shot him. Do you think I'll ever wake up? Maybe when your friends come with their pop-guns. . . .

OLGA. They won't touch you while you're here.

HUGO. You talked them into that? (*He pours out a glass of wine.*) I'll have to go out some time.

OLGA. Wait. You have the night. All sorts of things can happen in a night.

HUGO. What do you expect can happen?

OLGA. Things could change.

HUGO. What?

OLGA. You. Me.

HUGO. You?

OLGA. It depends on you.

HUGO (*he laughs, looks at her, and shrugs his shoulders*). Well?

OLGA. Why don't you come back to us?

HUGO (*laughing again*). Hell of a fine time to ask me that.

OLGA. But supposing it were possible? Supposing everything happened because of a misunderstanding? Haven't you ever wondered what you'd do, when you got out of prison?

HUGO. No.

OLGA. What did you think about?

HUGO. About what I did. I tried to understand why I did it.

OLGA. And did you? (HUGO *shrugs his shoulders*.) How did it all happen, you and Hoederer? Was it true he was hanging around Jessica?

HUGO. Yes.

OLGA. Then you were jealous?

HUGO. I don't know. I . . . I don't think so.

OLGA. Tell me.

HUGO. What?

OLGA. Everything. From the beginning.

HUGO. It won't be difficult; it's a story I know by heart; I used to go over it every day in prison. But what it all means, that's something else. If you look at it from a distance, it holds together after a fashion; but if you try to analyse it, it blows up in your face. The fact remains I fired the shots. . . .

OLGA. Begin at the beginning.

HUGO. The beginning? You know it as well as I do. Anyway, was there ever a beginning? You can begin the story in March forty-three, when Louis sent for me. Or you can begin it the year before when I joined the Party. Or before that, when I was born. Anyway, let's take it that the whole thing began in March nineteen-forty-three. . . .

As he is talking the lights dim down little by little.

Curtain

Scene One

The scene is OLGA'S *flat, two years earlier. It is night. Through the door at the back, can be heard the sound of voices, a murmur that grows and fades, as though several people were talking vehemently.*

    HUGO *is typing. He seems much younger than in the preceding scene.* IVAN *is walking up and down.*

IVAN. I say!

HUGO. Eh?

IVAN. Can't you stop typing?

HUGO. Why?

IVAN. Makes me nervous.

HUGO. You don't look the nervous type.

IVAN. Don't suppose so. Just now, it upsets me. Couldn't you talk to me?

HUGO (*delighted*). Of course. What's your name?

IVAN. My pseudonym's Ivan. What's yours?

HUGO. Raskolnikoff.

IVAN (*laughing*). That's a name and a half.

HUGO. It's my Party name.

IVAN. Where did you dig that one up?

HUGO. It's the name of a chap in a book.

IVAN. What did he do?

HUGO. He killed someone.

IVAN. Oh! Have you killed someone?

HUGO. No. (*Pause.*) Who sent you here?

IVAN. Louis.

HUGO. What did he tell you to do?

IVAN. Wait until ten o'clock.

HUGO. And then?

Gesture from IVAN *to show that* HUGO *mustn't ask him. Sound of voices from the adjoining room. It sounds like an argument.*

IVAN. What the hell are they up to, in there?

Gesture from HUGO, *imitating* IVAN, *to show that he mustn't be questioned.*

HUGO. Trouble is, this conversation can't get very far. (*Pause.*)

IVAN. Been with the Party long?

HUGO. Since 'forty-two, just about a year. I joined when the Regent declared war on the U.S.S.R. . . . What about you?

IVAN. Can't remember. Suppose I've always been a member. (*Pause.*) Are you the one who prints the newspapers?

HUGO. I and others.

IVAN. It comes my way quite often, but I don't read it. It's not your fault, but your news is always a week behind Moscow Radio or the B.B.C.

HUGO. What do you expect? We get our news by listening to the radio, like everyone else.

IVAN. I'm not complaining. You do your job—that's all there is to it. (*Pause.*) What's the time?

HUGO. Five to ten. (IVAN *yawns.*) What's the matter?

IVAN. Nothing.

HUGO. Don't you feel well?

IVAN. I'm all right. I'm always like this *before*.

HUGO. Before what?

IVAN. Before nothing. (*Pause.*) When I'm on my bike, I feel better. (*Pause.*) I feel such a harmless chap. I wouldn't hurt a fly. (*He yawns.*)

OLGA comes in by the front door. She puts a suitcase down near the door.

OLGA (*to* IVAN). There you are. Will it fit on your carrier?

IVAN. Let's see. Yes, that's okay.

OLGA. It's ten o'clock. Off you go. You've been told about the road-block and the house?

IVAN. Yes.

OLGA. Good luck.

IVAN. (*Pause.*) Aren't you going to kiss me?

OLGA. Of course. (*She kisses him on both cheeks.*)

IVAN (*goes to pick up the suitcase, then turns round in the doorway and jokingly to* HUGO). So long, Raskolnikoff.

HUGO (*smiling*). Go to hell.

> IVAN *goes out.*

OLGA. You shouldn't have told him to go to hell.

HUGO. Why not?

OLGA. You shouldn't say such things.

HUGO (*surprised*). You aren't superstitious, are you?

OLGA (*annoyed*). Of course not.

HUGO (*he looks at her carefully*). What's he going to do?

OLGA. You don't have to know.

HUGO. He's going to blow up the bridge at Korsk.

OLGA. Why do you want me to tell you? In case of accidents, the less you know, the better.

HUGO. But you know what he's going to do?

OLGA (*shrugging her shoulders*). Oh, I. . . .

HUGO. Of course; you'd hold your tongue. You're like Louis; they could kill you before you'd speak. (*Short silence.*) What proof have you that I would talk? How can you trust me if you don't put me to the test?

OLGA. The Party isn't a set of evening classes. We don't try and test you. We try and use you to the best advantage.

HUGO (*pointing to the typewriter*). And that's my advantage?

OLGA. Would you know how to unbuckle railway-lines?

HUGO. No.

OLGA. Well? (*Pause.* HUGO *looks at himself in the mirror.*)
Admiring yourself?

HUGO. I'm looking to see if I'm like my father. (*Pause.*) If I
had a moustache, you couldn't tell us apart.

OLGA (*shrugging her shoulders*). So what?

HUGO. I don't like my father.

OLGA. We know.

HUGO. He said to me: 'In my young days, I belonged to a
revolutionary group too. I wrote articles for their paper.
You'll get over it, as I did. . . .'

OLGA. Why are you telling me this?

HUGO. For no reason. I think of it every time I look in a mirror,
that's all.

OLGA (*looking at the door of the meeting-place*). Is Louis in
there?

HUGO. Yes.

OLGA. And Hoederer?

HUGO. I don't know him, but I suppose so. Who exactly is he?

OLGA. He was a member of the Landstag before it was dis-
solved. Now he's the secretary of the Party.

HUGO. They're making enough noise in there. Sounds as if
they're quarrelling.

OLGA. Hoederer called a committee meeting to vote on a
proposition.

HUGO. What proposition?

OLGA. I don't know. All I know is that Louis is against it.

HUGO (*smiling*). Well, if he's against it, so am I. No need to
know what it's all about. (*Pause.*) Olga, you've got to help me.

OLGA. What about?

HUGO. To convince Louis he must let me take part in a direct
action. I'm sick of doing nothing but write while the boys
are risking their lives.

OLGA. You run risks too.

HUGO. It's not the same. (*Pause.*) Olga, I don't want to go on
living.

OLGA. Really ? Why ?

HUGO. Too difficult.

OLGA. You're married, aren't you ?

HUGO. Bah!

OLGA. Don't you love your wife ?

HUGO. Yes, of course. (*Pause.*) A chap who doesn't want to live should be useful, if one knew how to use him. (*Pause. Shouts and murmurs from the room where the meeting is being held.*) Seems to be going badly in there.

OLGA (*worried*). Very badly.

The door opens, LOUIS *comes out with two men, who quickly cross to the front door, open it and exit.*

LOUIS. It's over.

OLGA. Where's Hoederer ?

LOUIS. Went out the back way with Boris and Lucas.

OLGA. Well ?

LOUIS (*shrugs his shoulders without replying. Pause*). The bastards !

OLGA. Have you voted ?

LOUIS. Yes. (*Pause.*) He's authorized to open negotiations. Next time he arrives with definite offers, he'll get his own way.

OLGA. When's your next meeting ?

LOUIS. In ten days' time. Gives us a week. (OLGA *points at* HUGO.) What ? Oh yes. . . . Are you still here ? (*He looks at* HUGO *and repeats, absent-mindedly.*) Still here . . . (HUGO *makes a movement to go.*) Wait a minute. I may have a job for you. (*To* OLGA.) You know him better than I do. How good is he ?

OLGA. He'll get by.

LOUIS. You don't think he'd crack up ?

OLGA. I'm sure not. He's more likely to . . .

LOUIS. What ?

OLGA. Nothing. He's all right.

LOUIS. Okay. (*Pause.*) Ivan gone?

OLGA. Quarter of an hour ago.

LOUIS. We've got a ringside seat; we'll hear the explosion. (*Pause. He comes back to* HUGO.) They tell me you're asking for action?

HUGO. Yes.

LOUIS. Why?

HUGO. I'm like that.

LOUIS. Fine. Trouble is, you don't know how to do anything with your ten fingers.

HUGO. In Russia, at the end of the last century, there were chaps who watched for the arrival of some grand-duke, with a bomb in their pockets. The bomb went off, blew the grand-duke to hell, and the poor chap with him. I can do that.

LOUIS. They were anarchists. You dream about them, because that's what you are, an intellectual anarchist. You're fifty years behind the times.

HUGO. Then I'm an incompetent.

LOUIS. In that line of country, yes.

HUGO. Okay.

LOUIS. Wait. (*Pause.*) I may perhaps find a job for you.

HUGO. A real job? You'd really trust me?

LOUIS. We'll see. Sit down. (*Pause.*) Here's the situation; on one side we've got the Fascist government of the Regent with its political line based on the Axis; on the other side is our Party, fighting for liberty and a classless society. Between the two, the Pentagon representing the liberal bourgeoisie and the nationalists. Three groups with irreconcilable interests, three groups of men who hate each other. (*Pause.*) Hoederer called this meeting tonight because he wants the Proletarian Party to join with the Fascists and the Pentagon, and form a Coalition Government to take power after the war. What d'you say to that?

HUGO (*smiling*). You're pulling my leg.

LOUIS. Why?

HUGO. Because it's ridiculous.

LOUIS. That's what we've been discussing for the last three hours. What would *you* do if the majority had declared itself in *favour* of this reconciliation?

HUGO. Are you asking me seriously?

LOUIS. Yes.

HUGO. I left my family and my friends the day I understood the meaning of the word oppression. In no circumstances would I agree to compromise with them. (*Pause.*) The whole thing's a joke, surely?

LOUIS. The Committee accepted Hoederer's proposition by four votes to three. In the coming week, Hoederer will meet the Regent's emissaries.

HUGO. Has he been bribed?

LOUIS. I don't know and I don't give a damn. *Objectively*, he's a traitor. That's enough for me.

HUGO. But, Louis . . . I mean, I don't know, but . . . but it's absurd. The Regent hates us, he sets traps for us, he's fighting against the U.S.S.R. alongside Germany, he's had our people shot. How could he. . . .?

LOUIS. The Regent has lost his belief in the victory of the Axis; he wants to save his skin. If the Allies win, he wants to be able to say he was playing a double game.

HUGO. But our boys. . . .

LOUIS. The whole of the P.A.C., which I represent, is against Hoederer. But you know what it is; the Proletarian Party was born from the fusion of the P.A.C. and the Social-democrats. The Social-democrats voted for Hoederer, and they're in the majority.

HUGO. Why did they. . . .?

LOUIS. Because Hoederer frightens them. . . .

HUGO. Can't we get rid of them?

LOUIS. A party split? Impossible. (*Pause.*) Hugo, are you really with us?

HUGO. You and Olga have taught me all I know, and I owe you everything. For me, you are the Party.

LOUIS (*to* OLGA). Does he believe what he says?

OLGA. Yes.

LOUIS. Fine. (*To* HUGO.) You understand the situation; we can neither walk out, nor force this through the committee. But it's nothing more nor less than one of Hoederer's manoeuvres. Without Hoederer, we've got the others in our pockets. (*Pause.*) Last Tuesday, Hoederer asked the Party to find him a secretary. A married student.

HUGO. Why married?

LOUIS. I don't know. You married?

HUGO. Yes.

LOUIS. Well then? You accept? (*They look at each other a moment.*)

HUGO (*with conviction*). Yes.

LOUIS. Very good. You'll leave tomorrow, with your wife. He's living twenty miles away, in a country house some friend has lent him. He lives with three thugs who're there in case of accidents. You've only got to watch him; we'll make contact with you as soon as you arrive. He mustn't be allowed to meet the Regent's envoys. Or, at least, he mustn't meet them twice. Understand?

HUGO. Yes.

LOUIS. The night we give you the word, you'll open the door to three comrades who'll do the job. They'll have a car, and you can get away with your wife while they're at it.

HUGO. So that's it! That's all it is. Is that all you think me capable of?

LOUIS. Don't you agree?

HUGO. No. Not in the least. I don't want to be your cat's-paw. We intellectuals have our pride too, you know. We can't take on just any kind of job.

OLGA. Hugo!

HUGO. Now listen to me. Here's my proposal. No contacts, no spying. I'll do the job myself.

LOUIS. You?

HUGO. Yes.

LOUIS. It's too tough for an amateur.

HUGO. Your three killers may run into Hoederer's bodyguard; they might quite easily be killed. If I'm his secretary, and if I win his confidence, I'll be alone with him several hours a day.

LOUIS (*hesitatingly*). I don't. . . .

OLGA. Louis!

LOUIS. Well?

OLGA (*gently*). Trust him. He's a kid looking for a break. He won't let you down.

LOUIS. Are you going bail for him?

OLGA. Certainly.

LOUIS. Very well. Now listen. . . .

Dull explosion in the distance.

OLGA. He's done it!

LOUIS. Put out the light.

They put out the lights and open the window. Far away, the glow of a fire.

OLGA. It's burning nicely. Very nicely. Quite a bonfire. He's brought it off.

They are all at the window.

HUGO. He's brought it off. Before the week's out, you'll both be here, on a night like this, waiting for news. You'll be worried, and you'll talk of me, and I'll be important to you. You'll be wondering: how has he got on? Then the telephone will ring, or someone will knock at the door, and you'll smile, as you're smiling now, and you'll say: 'He's brought it off. . . .'

Curtain

Scene Two

The studio.

This is a self-contained building in the garden of the villa belonging to Hoederer.

A bed, cupboards, armchairs, chairs. Female garments scattered all over the furniture, the bed covered with suitcases.

JESSICA *is unpacking. She looks out of the window, then goes to a closed suitcase standing in a corner (initials* H.B.*), pulls it down-stage, takes a look out of the window again, goes to a man's suit hanging in a cupboard, searches through it quickly, finds something she looks at, with her back to the audience, glances again at the window. She shuts the suitcase quickly, puts the key back in the pocket of the jacket, and hides under the mattress the objects she was holding in her hand.*

HUGO *enters.*

HUGO. I thought they were never going to stop. Were you bored without me?

JESSICA. Horribly.

HUGO. What did you do with yourself?

JESSICA. I've been to sleep.

HUGO. You can't have been bored if you were asleep.

JESSICA. I dreamed I was bored and woke myself up, so I unpacked. (*She gestures to the clothes piled pell-mell on the bed and the chairs.*)

HUGO. So I see.

JESSICA. What's he like?

HUGO. Who?

JESSICA. Hoederer.

HUGO. Hoederer? Very ordinary.

JESSICA. How old is he?

HUGO. Between two ages.

JESSICA. Which two?

HUGO. Twenty and sixty.

JESSICA. Is he tall or short?

HUGO. Middling.

JESSICA. Any distinguishing marks?

HUGO. A livid scar, a glass eye and a wig.

JESSICA. You're teasing me and trying to be clever. You know quite well you couldn't describe him.

HUGO. Yes, I could.

JESSICA. No, you couldn't. What colour are his eyes?

HUGO. Grey.

JESSICA. Honey-bee, you think everyone's eyes are grey. People have blue eyes, brown eyes, green eyes, black eyes. Some people even have mauve eyes. What colour are mine? (*She hides her eyes with her hand.*) Don't look.

HUGO. Blue.

JESSICA. You looked.

HUGO. No, I didn't. You told me this morning.

JESSICA. Idiot. (*She goes up to him.*) Hugo—try and remember. Has he got a moustache?

HUGO. No. (*Pause. Firmly.*) I'm sure he hasn't.

JESSICA (*sadly*). I wish I could believe you.

HUGO (*thinks hard, then asserts*). He was wearing a spotted tie.

JESSICA. Spotted?

HUGO. With spots.

JESSICA. Bah!

HUGO. The kind . . . (*he makes the gesture of tying a bow-tie.*) You know.

JESSICA. I knew it! I knew it! All the time he was talking to you—you looked at his tie. Hugo—he frightened you!

HUGO. Of course he didn't!

JESSICA. He frightened you!

HUGO. He isn't frightening.

JESSICA. Then why did you look at his tie?

HUGO. I didn't want to frighten him.

JESSICA. I see. All right, honey-bee. I'll look at him, and when you want to know what he's like, just ask me. What did he say?

HUGO. I told him my father was vice-president of the Tosk Coal Mines, and we quarrelled when I joined the Party.

JESSICA. What did he say?

HUGO. Fine.

JESSICA. And then?

HUGO. I told him quite frankly I had taken my degree, but I made him understand I wasn't an intellectual—that I wasn't ashamed to work as a copyist; that I made it a point of honour to conform to obedience and the strictest discipline.

JESSICA. And what did he say to that?

HUGO. Fine.

JESSICA. And that took you two hours?

HUGO. There were pauses.

JESSICA. You always tell me what you say to other people, but never what other people say to you.

HUGO. That's because I think you're more interested in me than in other people.

JESSICA. Of course, my darling. But I know you already. I don't know the others.

HUGO. Do you want to know Hoederer?

JESSICA. I want to know everybody.

HUGO. Hum! He's common.

JESSICA. How do you know? You never looked at him.

HUGO. You've got to be common to wear spotted ties.

JESSICA. The Greek empresses slept with their barbarian generals.

HUGO. There weren't any Empresses in Greece.

JESSICA. There were in Byzantium.

HUGO. There were barbarian generals and Greek empresses in Byzantium, but we have no record of what they did together.

JESSICA. What else could they do? (*A tiny pause.*) Did he ask you what I was like?

HUGO. No.

JESSICA. You wouldn't have been able to tell him, anyway. You don't know.

HUGO. No. Besides it's too late for you to worry about him.

JESSICA. Why?

HUGO. You'll hold your tongue?

JESSICA. With both hands.

HUGO. He's going to die.

JESSICA. Is he ill?

HUGO. No, but he's going to be assassinated. Like all political figures.

JESSICA. Oh. (*Pause.*) What about you, honey-bee? Are you a political figure too?

HUGO. Certainly.

JESSICA. And what should the widow of a political figure do?

HUGO. She joins her husband's party and carries on his work.

JESSICA. Heavens! I'd rather kill myself on his grave.

HUGO. That isn't done nowadays, except in Malabar.

JESSICA. All right, then this is what I'll do. I'll go to your assassins, one by one. I'll make them fall madly in love with me, and when they finally think they can console my haughty and grieving spirit, I'll plunge a knife into their black hearts.

HUGO. Which would you enjoy more? Killing them or seducing them?

JESSICA. You're stupid and vulgar.

HUGO. Are we playing or not?

JESSICA. We're not playing any more. Let me unpack.

HUGO. Don't bother about it now.

JESSICA. It's all done, except yours. Give me the keys.

HUGO. I gave them to you.

JESSICA (*pointing to the suitcase she opened at the beginning of the scene*). Not that one.

HUGO. I'll unpack it myself.

JESSICA. That's not your job, my soul.

HUGO. Since when is it yours? Are you playing at being domesticated?

JESSICA. You're playing at being a revolutionary.

HUGO. Revolutionaries don't need domesticated women.

JESSICA. Revolutionaries prefer brunettes, like your beloved Olga.

HUGO. Jealous?

JESSICA. I'd like to be. I've never played at that. Shall we play it now?

HUGO. If you like.

JESSICA. All right. Give me the key!

HUGO. Never!

JESSICA. What's in that suitcase?

HUGO. A shameful secret.

JESSICA. What secret?

HUGO. I am not the son of my father.

JESSICA. How delighted you would be, my angel! But it's impossible, you look too much like him.

HUGO. It's not true! Jessica! Do you really think I'm like him?

JESSICA. Are we playing or not?

HUGO. We're playing.

JESSICA. Open that case.

HUGO. I have sworn never to open it.

JESSICA. It's stuffed with letters from your love—or maybe photographs? Open it!

HUGO. Never!

JESSICA. Open it, open it!

HUGO. No, no and no.

JESSICA. You're playing?

HUGO. Yes.

JESSICA. All right, pax. I'm not playing any more. Open it.

HUGO. Non pax. I shan't.

JESSICA. I don't mind. I know what's in it.

HUGO. What?

JESSICA. This . . . this . . . (*She puts her hand under the mattress, then holds her hands behind his back and flourishes the photographs.*) These!

HUGO. Jessica!

JESSICA (*triumphantly*). I found the key in your blue suit. I know who is your mistress, your princess, your empress. It isn't me, it isn't your brunette, it's you yourself, my darling, it's you yourself. Twelve photographs of yourself in your case.

HUGO. Give them back.

JESSICA. Twelve pictures of your dreamy youth. At three, at six, at eight, at twelve, at sixteen. You took them when your father turned you out. They've followed you everywhere; how you must love yourself.

HUGO. Jessica, I'm not playing now.

JESSICA. When you were six you wore a stiff collar. It must have scratched your skinny little neck, and you had a velvet suit with a bow-tie!

HUGO (*who has been pretending to give up, suddenly springs at her*). Give them to me, you little devil! Give them to me.

JESSICA. Let me go! (*They fall on to the bed.*) Look out—you'll kill us both.

HUGO. Give them to me!

JESSICA. I tell you it'll go off! (HUGO *gets up. She shows the revolver she has been holding behind her back.*) I found that too.

HUGO. Give it to me.

> He takes it from her, goes to the pocket of his suit, takes the key, opens the suitcase, picks up the photographs and puts them with the revolver back in the suitcase. Pause.

JESSICA. What's that revolver for?

HUGO. I always carry one.

JESSICA. That's not true. You never had one before you came here. Why have you got a gun?

HUGO. Do you want to know?

JESSICA. Yes, but tell me seriously. You've no right to keep me out of your life.

HUGO. You won't tell a soul?

JESSICA. No one in the world.

HUGO. I'm going to kill Hoederer.

JESSICA. You're maddening, Hugo. I told you I wasn't playing any more.

HUGO. Ha! Ha! Am I playing? Am I serious? Mystery. . . .

JESSICA. Why do you want to kill him? You don't even know him.

HUGO. So that my wife will take me seriously.

JESSICA. I'd adore you, I'd hide you, I'd feed you, I'd look after you in your hiding place. When we had been denounced by our neighbours, I should rush through the soldiers and take you in my arms, crying madly, 'I love you. . . .'

HUGO. Tell me now.

JESSICA. What?

HUGO. That you love me.

JESSICA. I love you.

HUGO. Say it properly.

JESSICA. I love you.

HUGO. That's not properly.

JESSICA. What's the matter with you? Are you playing?

HUGO. No. I'm not playing.

JESSICA. Then why do you ask me like that? You don't usually.

HUGO. I don't know. I'd like to think you love me. It's my right, isn't it? Then say so. Say so really and truly.

JESSICA. I love you. I love you. No. I love you. Oh, go to hell. How would you say it?

HUGO. I love you.

JESSICA. You see. You can't do it any better than I can.

HUGO. Jessica, you don't believe what I just told you.

JESSICA. That you loved me?

HUGO. That I am going to kill Hoederer.

JESSICA. Of course I believe you.

HUGO. Jessica, try to understand. Be serious.

JESSICA. Why should I be serious?

HUGO. Because we can't play all the time.

JESSICA. I don't like being serious, but I'll try. I'll play at being serious.

HUGO. Look me in the eyes. No. Don't laugh. Listen. It's true about Hoederer. The Party has sent me.

JESSICA. I knew it. Why didn't you tell me before?

HUGO. You might have refused to come with me.

JESSICA. Why? It's your business. It doesn't concern me.

HUGO. It's a funny job, you know. . . . He looks a tough sort of egg.

JESSICA. We'll chloroform him and tie him to the mouth of a cannon.

HUGO. Jessica! I'm serious.

JESSICA. So am I.

HUGO. No, you're playing at being serious. You said so.

JESSICA. No, you said so.

HUGO. You must believe me—please, you must believe me.

JESSICA. I'll believe you if you'll believe I'm being serious.

HUGO. All right. I believe you.

JESSICA. No. You're playing at believing me.

HUGO. God give me patience! Jessica . . . (*Knock at the door.*) Come in!

> JESSICA *stands in front of the suitcase with her back to the audience, while* HUGO *opens the door.* SLICK *and* GEORGES *enter, smiling. Sub-machine guns and revolvers in their belts.*
>
> *Pause.*

GEORGES. Hullo.

HUGO. Yes?

GEORGES. We've come to give you a hand.

HUGO. What for?

SLICK. Unpacking.

JESSICA. It's very nice of you, but I can manage.

SLICK (*taking a petticoat from the back of a chair, and holding it at arm's length*). Fold these things in the middle, don't you?

GEORGES. Hands off, Slick. Might give you ideas. You must excuse him, ma'am; we haven't seen a woman for six months.

SLICK. Couldn't even remember what they were like.

They look at her.

JESSICA. Is it coming back to you?

GEORGES. Yeh. Bit by bit.

JESSICA. Aren't there any girls in the village?

SLICK. Maybe. We don't get out.

GEORGES. The last secretary climbed the wall every night—so one morning we found him with his head in a pond. The old man decided the next one must bring his wife and get his relaxation at home.

JESSICA. Very thoughtful of him.

SLICK. Doesn't seem to think we need relaxation too.

JESSICA. Why not?

GEORGES. He says he wants to keep us wild.

HUGO. They are Hoederer's bodyguard.

JESSICA. D'you know I had guessed?

SLICK (*meaning his machine-gun*). Because of this?

JESSICA. Because of that too.

GEORGES. Don't think we're professionals, will you? I'm a plumber by trade. We're doing this as a special job, for the Party.

SLICK. Not afraid of us, are you?

JESSICA. Of course not. But I'd rather you put your decorations down. Put them in the corner.

GEORGES. Sorry.

SLICK. Can't be done.

JESSICA. Don't you even put them down to sleep!

GEORGES. No, ma'am.

HUGO. When I went in to see Hoederer, they pushed me along with the muzzles of their guns in my back.

GEORGES (*laughing*). That's what we're like.

SLICK (*laughing*). One little slip and you'd have been a widow. (*Everyone laughs.*)

JESSICA. Your boss must be very frightened.

SLICK. He isn't frightened, but he doesn't want to be knocked off.

JESSICA. Why should he be killed?

SLICK. How should I know? All I know is someone wants to kill him. His pals came and warned him, nearly a fortnight ago.

JESSICA. How perfectly fascinating.

GEORGES. We're on guard, that's all. Oh! You'll get used to it. It's not much to look at. (*He is wandering round the room with an air of false negligence. When he gets to the cupboard, he opens it and brings out* HUGO'S *suit.*) Gee, what an outfit! Watch for moths! (*Pretending to brush it, he feels the pockets of the suit, then puts it back in the cupboard.* JESSICA *and* HUGO *look at each other.*)

JESSICA. Why don't we all sit down?

SLICK. No. No, thanks.

JESSICA. Do you mind if I do? (*She and* HUGO *sit down.*)

SLICK (*going to the window*). Nice view.

GEORGES. Comfortable place.

SLICK. Nice and quiet.

GEORGES. Seen the bed? Big enough for three.

SLICK. For four—newly weds don't take up much room.

GEORGES. All that waste space, when some people have to sleep on the floor.

SLICK. Shut up—you'll make me dream about it tonight.

JESSICA. Have you got beds?

GEORGES (*pointing to* SLICK). He sleeps on the carpet in the office, I sleep in the corridor outside the old man's door.

JESSICA. Isn't it very uncomfortable?

GEORGES. It would be for your husband—he looks the delicate type. It's all right for us. Trouble is, we've got no place of our own. The garden isn't healthy, so we have to spend our time in the hall.

SLICK *bends down and looks under the bed.*

HUGO. What are you looking for?
SLICK. Rats. (*He gets up.*)
HUGO. Did you see any?
SLICK. No.
HUGO. I'm glad. (*Pause.*)
JESSICA. So you've left your boss all alone? Aren't you afraid something may happen to him if you stay away too long?
GEORGES. Leon has stopped with him. (*Pointing to the telephone.*) If anything was up, he could always give us a ring.

Pause. HUGO *gets up, pale with nervousness.* JESSICA *gets up also.* HUGO *goes to the door and opens it.*

HUGO. Well, come along any time. You'll always be welcome.
GEORGES (*goes to door calmly and closes it*). We're going. In a minute. Just a formality.
HUGO. What formality?
SLICK. Got to search the room.
HUGO. No.
GEORGES. No?
HUGO. You'll do nothing of the sort.
GEORGES. Don't get excited. It's orders.
HUGO. Whose orders?
SLICK. Hoederer's.
HUGO. Hoederer ordered you to search my room?
GEORGES. Come on now, master-mind, don't play the fool. We've been warned; someone's going to pull a gun one of these days. You don't think we're going to let anyone come here without going through his pockets? You might be

toting a couple of grenades, or some other fireworks, though I must say, you don't look the type.

HUGO. I asked if Hoederer had specifically ordered you to search my belongings.

SLICK (*to* GEORGES). Specifically?

GEORGES. Specifically.

SLICK. No one comes in here without being frisked. It's orders.

HUGO. And I refuse to be searched. I'll be the exception that proves the rule. That's all.

GEORGES. Don't you belong to the Party?

HUGO. Of course.

GEORGES. Then what did they teach you back there? Don't you know what an order is?

HUGO. I know as well as you do.

GEORGES. And when you're given an order, don't you know you've got to carry it out?

HUGO. Of course I know.

GEORGES. Well, then?

HUGO. I obey orders, but I have my self-respect. I don't obey idiotic orders that are only given to make me look ridiculous.

GEORGES. D'you hear, Slick? Have you any self-respect?

SLICK. Don't think so. What about you, Georges?

GEORGES. You've got to have education before you can have self-respect.

HUGO. Don't you understand? If I joined the Party it was to ensure that one day all men should have the right to respect themselves.

GEORGES. Make him stop, Slick, or I'll burst into tears. We're different, master-mind. We joined the Party because we were fed up with starving.

SLICK. And so that one day all the other bastards like us should get enough to eat.

GEORGES. Stop chewing the rag, Slick. Open that for a start.

HUGO. You shan't touch a thing.

GEORGES. Won't I, master-mind? How are you going to stop me?

HUGO. If you lay a finger on anything of mine, we leave the villa tonight, and Hoederer can look for a new secretary.

GEORGES. Gee, you're frightening me!

HUGO. All right, then, search, if you're not afraid.

GEORGES *scratches his head.* JESSICA, *who has remained very calm during the whole scene, goes to them.*

JESSICA. Why not telephone to Hoederer?

GEORGES. To Hoederer?

JESSICA. He'll tell you what to do.

GEORGES *and* SLICK *consult each other with a look.*

GEORGES. Could be. (*He goes to the telephone, rings and picks up the receiver.*) Hullo, Leon? Tell the old man this half-wit won't let us get on with the job. What? Oh, a lot of hot air. (*To* SLICK.) He's gone to ask.

SLICK. Okay. But I'll tell you one thing, Georges. I'm fond of the old man, but if he takes it into his head to make an exception for this bourgeois bastard, when you think we've frisked everyone who comes near the place, including the postman—I'm chucking in my hand.

GEORGES. I'm with you there. Either we search the place, or we're the ones who go.

SLICK. Maybe I have no self-respect, but I have my pride like anyone else.

HUGO. You may be right, Goliath; but if Hoederer himself gives the order to search, I shall still leave this house five minutes later.

HOEDERER *enters.*

HOEDERER. What's all this about?

SLICK *falls back a step.*

SLICK. He won't let us search him.

HOEDERER. No?

HUGO. If you allow them to search me, I go. That's all.

HOEDERER. I see.

GEORGES. If you don't let us search him, we're going.

HOEDERER. Sit down. (*They sit down, ill-humouredly.*) By the way, Hugo, no formality. We're all friends here. (*He picks up a slip and pair of stockings from the back of a chair, and makes to carry them over to the bed.*)

JESSICA. Thank you. (*She takes them from him, rolls them up into a ball, and without moving, throws them on to the bed.*)

HOEDERER. What's your name?

JESSICA. Jessica.

HOEDERER (*looking at her*). I thought you would be ugly.

JESSICA. I'm sorry.

HOEDERER (*still looking at her*). Yes. It's a pity. Were they quarrelling over you?

JESSICA. Not yet.

HOEDERER. Don't let that happen. (*He sits in an arm-chair.*) This question of the search, it doesn't matter.

SLICK. We. . . .

HOEDERER. Doesn't matter at all. We'll talk about it later. (*To* SLICK.) What's he done? What do you accuse him of? Is he too well-dressed? He talks like a book?

SLICK. He's not our class.

HOEDERER. We leave all that outside. (*He looks at them.*) You've started out badly. (*To* HUGO.) You were insolent because you are weaker than they are. (*To* SLICK *and* GEORGES.) You were bad-tempered this morning, and you took it out on him. The next thing, you'll start playing tricks on him, and in a week, when I need him to take a letter, you'll tell me you've had to fish him out of the pond.

HUGO. Not if I can help it. . . .

HOEDERER. You can't help anything. Things mustn't get to that pitch, that's all. Four men who live together, either get along, or cut each other's throats. You'll be good enough to get along.

GEORGES (*with dignity*). A man can't be responsible for his feelings.

HOEDERER (*with emphasis*). Certainly he can. Particularly when he's on duty, with members of the same Party.

GEORGES. We don't belong to the same Party.

HOEDERER (*to* HUGO). Aren't you one of us ?

HUGO. Certainly.

HOEDERER. Well ?

GEORGES. We may belong to the same Party, but we didn't join for the same reasons.

HOEDERER. Everyone joins for the same reasons.

GEORGES. Pardon me. He joined to teach poor people the respect they owe themselves.

HOEDERER. Nonsense.

SLICK. That's what he said.

HUGO. And you joined to get a square meal. That's what you said.

HOEDERER. Well then ? You're both agreed.

SLICK. What ?

HOEDERER. Slick! Didn't you tell him that you were ashamed of being hungry ? (*He bends towards* SLICK *and waits for an answer that does not come.*) That it made you mad because you couldn't think of anything else ? That a lad of twenty can do better than spend all his time thinking about his belly ?

SLICK. You didn't have to say that in front of him.

HOEDERER. Didn't you tell him all that ?

SLICK. What does that prove ?

HOEDERER. It proves that you wanted your grub and some-thing else besides. He calls that self-respect. You mustn't mind the words he uses. Everyone has the right to use the words he likes.

SLICK. It wasn't respect. It made me feel sick when he called it self-respect. He uses the words that come into his head; he thinks of everything with his head.

HUGO. What else do you want me to think with?

SLICK. When it's been chopped off, master-mind, you won't be able to think with your head. It's true I wanted it to stop, good God, yes. Only for a moment, a single moment, to be able to think about something else. Anything but myself. But that wasn't self-respect. You've never been hungry and you come to us to preach, like the lady visitors who came to see my mother when she was drunk and told her she had no self-respect.

HUGO. That's a lie.

GEORGES. Have you ever been hungry? You're the kind that has to take a walk before meals to get up an appetite.

HUGO. Just this once you're right. I don't know what it is to have an appetite. If you'd seen the tonics I took as a kid! I always left half my food behind—what a waste! So they made me open my mouth: they said, one for daddy, one for mummy, one for Aunty Anna. And they pushed the spoon down my throat. Do you know what happened? I grew. But I never got any fatter. That's when they made me drink fresh blood from the slaughter-house, because I had no colour. I've never eaten meat from that day to this. Every night my father used to say: 'The boy isn't hungry. . . .' Every night, can you imagine that? 'Eat, Hugo, eat: you'll make yourself ill.' They made me take cod-liver oil; that's the height of luxury; a drug to make you hungry, when there are people in the streets who would have sold themselves for a steak; I saw them from my windows, carrying banners: 'Give us bread'. Then I had to sit down at table. Eat, Hugo, eat. One for the night watchman, who is on strike, one for the old woman who picks scraps out of the dustbin, one for the carpenter with the broken leg. I left my home. I joined the Party, and all I heard was the same thing over again: 'You've never been hungry, Hugo, why do you interfere?

How can you understand? You've never been hungry.' No! I've never been hungry. Never! Never? Never! Maybe you can tell me what I must do to make you all stop reproaching me?

Pause.

HOEDERER. You heard him? All right. Tell him. Tell him what he must do, Slick! What do you suggest? Should he cut off a hand? Put out an eye? Give you his wife? What price must he pay for your forgiveness?

SLICK. I've nothing to forgive.

HOEDERER. Oh yes, you have: for joining the Party without being forced into it by poverty.

GEORGES. We don't reproach him. But there's a world between us: he's just an amateur. He joined because he thought it was a good idea, to make a gesture. We couldn't help ourselves.

HOEDERER. Do you think he could help himself? The hunger of others isn't easy to bear either.

GEORGES. Lots of people manage it quite well.

HOEDERER. That's because they have no imagination. The trouble with this boy is that he has too much.

SLICK. Okay. We don't want to hurt him. We don't like him, that's all. I suppose we have the right. . . .

HOEDERER. *What* right? You have *no* right. None. 'We don't like him . . .' You bastards, go and look at yourselves in the glass, and then come and explain your delicate sentiments if you have the courage. A man is judged by his work. Take care I don't judge you by yours—you've been slacking rather a lot lately.

HUGO (*crying out*). Don't try and defend me! Who asked you to make excuses for me? You can see it's no use; I'm used to it. When I saw them come in, just now, I recognized their expressions. They weren't very attractive. Believe me, they had come to make me pay for my father, and my grandfather, and my whole family who had always been able to eat their fill. I tell you I know them; they'll never be able to accept me. Thousands of them have looked at me with the same smile. I've fought. I've humiliated myself. I've done everything to make them forget. I've told them over and over again that I liked them, that I envied them, that I admired them. It was no use! No use! I'm the son of a rich father, an intellectual, a bastard who doesn't work with his hands. All right, let them think what they like. They are quite right. It's a question of class.

SLICK *and* GEORGES *look at each other in silence.*

HOEDERER *(to his bodyguard).* Well? (SLICK *and* GEORGES *shrug their shoulders uncomfortably.*) I shan't be any more careful of him than I am of you; you know I don't spare anyone. He doesn't work with his hands, but he'll have a tough time with me. (*Annoyed.*) To hell with all this. I've had enough.

GEORGES *(making up his mind).* Okay! (*To* HUGO.) It isn't that I like you. You can say what you like, there's something between us that'll never click. I don't say it's your fault, and it's true we didn't give you a break. I'll try not to make things tough for you. Okay?

HUGO *(limply).* Okay.

Pause.

HOEDERER *(tranquilly).* About this search. . . .

SLICK. Yes. The search . . . well, er. . . .

HOEDERER *(sharply).* Who asked you? (*To* HUGO, *going back to his ordinary voice.*) I trust you, my boy, but you must be a realist. If I make an exception for you today, tomorrow they'll ask me to make another, and it'll end up with a bastard blowing us all to glory because we didn't turn out his pockets. Supposing they ask you politely, now that you're all friends, would you let them search?

HUGO. I'm . . . afraid not.

HOEDERER. Oh! (*He looks at him.*) And if I asked you? (*Pause.*) I see. You've got your principles. I might make it a question of principle too. But principles and me . . . (*Pause.*) Look at me. Have you got a gun?

HUGO. No.

HOEDERER. Your wife?

HUGO. No.

HOEDERER. All right. I'll trust you. You two can go.

JESSICA. Wait. (*They turn round.*) Hugo, it would be wrong not to repay trust with trust.

HUGO. What?

JESSICA. You can search everything.

HUGO. But, Jessica. . . .

JESSICA. Why not? You'll make them believe you're hiding a revolver.

HUGO. Idiot!

JESSICA. Then why not let them? Your honour is satisfied. We're asking them.

GEORGES *and* SLICK *are still hesitating in the doorway.*

HOEDERER. Well? What are you waiting for? You heard her?

SLICK. We thought. . . .

HOEDERER. Don't think. Do as you're told.

SLICK. Okay, okay.

GEORGES. No point in wasting all that time. . . .

While they start to search, half-heartedly, HUGO *stares at* JESSICA *in stupefaction.*

HOEDERER (*to* SLICK *and* GEORGES). And let that teach you to trust other people. I always trust people. I trust everyone. (*They search.*) What are you doing? You must make a proper search, because they asked us to do it properly. Slick, look under the cupboard. That's right. Take out that suit. Feel it.

SLICK. I have.

HOEDERER. Then do it again. Look under the mattress. That's right. Slick, carry on. Georges, you come here. Frisk him. You only need feel his pockets. There. And his trouser pockets. That's right. And the revolver-pocket. Fine.

JESSICA. What about me?

HOEDERER. If you like. Georges. (GEORGES *doesn't move.*) What's the matter? Afraid of her?

GEORGES. It's all right!

> *He goes to* JESSICA, *very red in the face, and touches her with the tips of his fingers.* JESSICA *laughs.*

JESSICA. He's like a lady's maid.

> SLICK *has reached the suitcase which held the revolver.*

SLICK. Are the cases empty?

HUGO (*strained*). Yes.

HOEDERER (*looks at him carefully*). That one too?

SLICK (*picks it up*). No.

HUGO. Oh . . . no, not that one. I was just going to unpack it when you came in.

HOEDERER. Open it.

> SLICK *opens it and hunts through it.*

SLICK. Nothing here.

HOEDERER. Good. That's over. You may go.

SLICK (*to* HUGO). No hard feelings.

HUGO. No hard feelings.

JESSICA (*as they go out*). I'll come and see you in your hall.

> *They have gone.*

HOEDERER. If I were you, I wouldn't go too often.

JESSICA. Why not? I think they're sweet—especially Georges; he's such a baby.

HOEDERER. Hm! (*He goes to her.*) You're pretty, and that's a fact. You don't have to apologize. But, things being what they are, I can only see two alternatives. First, you'll be good to us all, if your heart is big enough.

JESSICA. It's very small.

HOEDERER. That's what I thought. Besides, they'd still manage to fight. There's only one solution: when your husband is out, lock the door and don't open to anyone, not even to me.

JESSICA. I see. Still, if you don't mind, I'll choose the third way.

HOEDERER. Just as you like. (*He bends towards her and breathes deeply.*) That's a wonderful scent. Don't use perfume when you visit the boys.

JESSICA. I never use scent.

HOEDERER. Pity. (*He turns and walks slowly to the middle of the room, then stops. During the scene his eyes dart everywhere. He is looking for something. From time to time, his gaze rests on* HUGO, *examining him.*) Well. There it is. (*Pause.*) There it is! (*Pause.*) Hugo, you report for duty tomorrow morning at ten o'clock.

HUGO. Yes, I know.

HOEDERER (*distrait, his eyes are ferreting everywhere*). Good. Good. Good. That's right. Everything's fine. All's well that ends well. You look very odd, standing there. Everything's all right; we're all friends again. Everyone's happy . . . (*Abruptly.*) You're tired, my boy.

HUGO. It's nothing. (HOEDERER *looks at him carefully.* HUGO *embarrassed, speaks with an effort.*) About that . . . that incident just now, I . . . I apologize.

HOEDERER (*without taking his eyes off* HUGO). I've forgotten it already.

HUGO. In future I won't give you any reason to complain. I will obey everything to the letter.

HOEDERER. You've already said that. Sure you aren't feeling ill? (HUGO *does not reply.*) If you were ill, there'd still be time to say so, and then I could ask the Committee to send someone else to take over from you.

HUGO. I'm not ill.

HOEDERER. Good. Well, I must leave you. You probably want to be alone, anyway. (*He goes to the table and looks at the books.*) Hegel, Marx, very good. Lorca, Thomas, Eliot: never heard of them. (*He flips through the books.*)

HUGO. They are poets.

HOEDERER (*picking up another book*). Poetry . . . poetry . . . more poetry. Do you write poems?

HUGO. N-no.

HOEDERER. Meaning, you used to. (*He goes away from the table, stops in front of the bed.*) A dressing-gown! You do yourself well. (*He offers him a cigarette.*)

HUGO (*refusing*). Thank you.

HOEDERER. Don't you smoke? (HUGO *shakes his head.*) Good. The Committee tells me you've never taken part in any direct action. Is that so?

HUGO. I was in charge of the newspaper.

HOEDERER. So I'm told. I haven't had a copy for two months. Before then you were editing it?

HUGO. Yes.

HOEDERER. You were doing a good job. So they gave up the services of such a good editor to send you to me?

HUGO. They thought I would suit you.

HOEDERER. Very kind of them. What about you? Are you glad you've left your old job?

HUGO. I. . . .

HOEDERER. That paper—it belonged to you. There were risks involved, responsibilities: in a sense, you might even call it direct action. (*He looks at* HUGO.) And now you're my secretary. (*Pause.*) Why did you give it all up? Why?

HUGO. I obey my orders.

HOEDERER. Don't talk about orders all the time. I'm very wary of people who talk about nothing else.

HUGO. I need discipline.

HOEDERER. I see. We'll probably get along. (*He puts his hand on* HUGO'S *shoulder.*) Listen. . . .

> HUGO *frees himself and jumps back.* HOEDERER *looks at him with renewed interest. His voice becomes hard and cutting.*

Ah? (*Pause.*) Ha! Ha!

HUGO. I . . . I don't like being touched.

HOEDERER (*in a hard quick voice*). When they searched that suitcase you were afraid: why?

HUGO. I wasn't afraid.

HOEDERER. I say you were afraid. What is in that case?

HUGO. Your men searched and found nothing.

HOEDERER. Nothing? We'll see. (*He goes to the case and opens it.*) They were looking for a gun. A gun can be hidden in a suitcase, but so can papers.

HUGO. Or strictly personal possessions.

HOEDERER. From the moment you come under my orders, get this into your head: you have no personal possessions. (*He rummages.*) Shirts, pants, everything new. Are you in the money?

HUGO. My wife has some.

HOEDERER. What on earth are these photos? (*He picks them up and looks at them. Pause.*) That's it. So that's it. (*He looks at another photo.*) A velvet suit . . . (*He looks at a third.*) A sailor collar and a beret. What a fine little gentleman!

HUGO. Give me those photos!

HOEDERER. Sh! (*He pushes him off.*) So that's what they were —your strictly personal possessions. You were afraid my boys would find them.

HUGO. If they had laid their filthy paws on them, if they had laughed when they looked at them . . . I . . .

HOEDERER. Well then, the mystery is solved! You see what it is to have a crime marked on your face; I would have sworn you were hiding at least a hand-grenade. (*He looks at the photos.*) You haven't changed. The skinny little legs . . . I can see you never had an appetite. You were so small they made you stand on a chair, you folded your arms and surveyed the world like a Napoleon. You didn't look very happy. No . . . it can't always be funny to be the son of rich people. It's a bad start in life. Why do you cart your past around if you want to bury it? (*Vague gesture from* HUGO.) You spend a great deal of time on yourself.

HUGO. I joined the Party to forget myself.

HOEDERER. And remind yourself every minute that you must forget. Well! We all have our own methods. (*He gives the photos back to* HUGO.) Hide them well. (HUGO *takes them and puts them in his inside pocket.*) See you in the morning, Hugo.

HUGO. Yes. Good night.

HOEDERER. Good night, Jessica.

JESSICA. Good night.

In the doorway, HOEDERER *turns.*

HOEDERER. Close the shutters and lock the door. You never know who may be in the garden. That's an order.

He goes out. HUGO *goes to the door and double-locks it.*

JESSICA. You were right. He is common. But he wasn't wearing a spotted tie.

HUGO. Where is the revolver?

JESSICA. I did enjoy that, honey-bee. It's the first time I've seen you up against real men.

HUGO. Jessica, where is the revolver?

JESSICA. My soul's delight, you don't know the rules of this game; what about the window? We can be seen from outside.

HUGO (*closes the shutters and comes back to her.*) Now?

JESSICA (*taking the revolver from her corsage*). When it comes to searching, Hoederer ought to have a woman too. I'm going to volunteer.

HUGO. When did you take it?

JESSICA. When you let in the watch-dogs.

HUGO. I thought they'd caught you in your own trap.

JESSICA. I nearly laughed in his face: 'I trust you! I trust
everybody. Let that teach you to trust people. . . .' What's
he thinking of? This confidence trick only works with men.

HUGO. Really?

JESSICA. You can hold your tongue, honey-bee. You were in
a fine state.

HUGO. Me? When?

JESSICA. When he told you he trusted you.

HUGO. I wasn't in a state.

JESSICA. Yes, you were.

HUGO. I wasn't.

JESSICA. If you ever leave me alone with a handsome man,
don't tell me you trust me, because I'm warning you: that
won't stop me deceiving you, if I want to. Just the opposite.

HUGO. I'm quite happy. I'd go off with my eyes shut.

JESSICA. Do you think you catch me with sentiments?

HUGO. No, my little statue of ice. I believe in the coldness of
the snow. The most burning seducer would freeze his
fingers. He'd caress you to warm you a little, and you would
melt between his hands.

JESSICA. Idiot; I'm not playing any more. (*A very short
silence.*) Were you very afraid?

HUGO. Just now? No. I don't think so. I watched them search,
and I thought: 'This is a game.' Nothing ever seems very
real to me.

JESSICA. Not even me?

HUGO. You. (*Looks at her for a moment, then turns his head
away.*) Tell me. Were you afraid too?

JESSICA. When I realized they were going to search me. I was
sure Georges would hardly touch me, but Slick would have
stripped me. I wasn't afraid he'd find the revolver; I was
afraid of his hands.

HUGO. I shouldn't have dragged you into this affair.

JESSICA. Don't you believe it. I've always wanted to have adventures.

HUGO. Jessica, this isn't a game. He's a dangerous man.

JESSICA. Dangerous? To whom?

HUGO. To the Party.

JESSICA. The Party? I thought he was the leader.

HUGO. He is *one* of the leaders. That's why . . .

JESSICA. Don't try to explain. I'll take your word.

HUGO. What do you believe?

JESSICA (*reciting*). I believe this man is dangerous, that he must be got rid of, and you have come to kill him. . . .

HUGO. Sh! (*Pause.*) Look at me. Sometimes I tell myself you are pretending to believe me, and you don't really believe me. Sometimes I think you really do believe. But you pretend not to believe. Which is true?

JESSICA (*laughing*). Nothing is true.

HUGO (*looking at her*). If I could read your mind . . .

JESSICA. Try.

HUGO (*shrugging his shoulders*). Bah! (*Pause.*) Dear God, I'm going to kill a man. I should feel the weight of that thought like a stone. There should be a great silence in my head. (*Crying out.*) Silence! (*Pause.*) Did you see how *solid* he was? How full of life? (*Pause.*) It's true! It's true! It's *true*! I'm really going to kill him; in a week's time he'll be lying on the ground with five bullets in his hide. (*Pause.*) What a game!

JESSICA (*beginning to laugh*). Poor little honey-bee, if you want to convince me you're an assassin, you must begin by convincing yourself.

HUGO. You don't think I look convinced?

JESSICA. Not in the least; you're playing your part very badly.

HUGO. But I'm not playing, Jessica.

JESSICA. Yes, you are. Besides, how could you kill him? I've got the revolver.

HUGO. Give it back to me.

JESSICA. Never, never, never! I won it. If it wasn't for me, you'd have lost it!

HUGO. Give me that gun.

JESSICA. No, I shan't. I'll go to Hoederer, and I'll say: I've come to make you happy, and while he is kissing me . . .

> HUGO, *who has pretended to give up, throws himself on her, in the same way as at the beginning of the scene. They fall on the bed, struggling, shouting and laughing.* HUGO *finally snatches the revolver, as the curtain falls, and she cries out:*

Look out! Look out! It'll go off!

Curtain

Scene Three

HOEDERER'S *office. Afternoon. Ten days later.*

An austere, but comfortable room. On the right, a desk. In the middle, a table loaded with books and pamphlets, covered by a carpet which reaches to the ground. At the side, on the left, a window is set on an angle, from which you can see the trees of the garden. Back right, a door. On the left of the door, a kitchen table with a gas-ring on it. Standing on this is a coffee-pot.

HUGO *is alone. He goes to the desk, picks up Hoederer's pen and looks at it. Then goes back to the gas-ring, picks up the coffee-pot and looks at it, whistling.* JESSICA *enters quietly.*

JESSICA. What are you doing?

HUGO (*puts the coffee-pot down quickly*). Jessica, you've been told not to come into the office.

JESSICA. What were you doing with that coffee-pot?

HUGO. What are you doing here?

JESSICA. I've come to see you, my soul.

HUGO. All right. You've seen me. Now run away! Hoederer is coming.

JESSICA. I was so bored without you, honey-bee.

HUGO. I've no time to play now, Jessica.

JESSICA (*looking round her*). Naturally, you didn't know how to describe anything. It smells of stale tobacco smoke, like my father's study, when I was little. It ought to be easy to describe the way a room smells.

HUGO. Listen to me . . .

JESSICA. Wait! (*She hunts for something in the pocket of her jacket.*) I came to bring you this.

HUGO. What?

JESSICA. This! You'd forgotten it.

HUGO. I hadn't forgotten it; I never carry it.

JESSICA. Exactly; you should never be without it.

HUGO. Jessica, you don't seem to understand. I've told you over and over again you're not to come here. If you want to play, there's the studio and the garden.

JESSICA. Hugo, you're talking to me as if I were six.

HUGO. Whose fault is that? It's quite unbearable; you can't look at me without laughing. It will be charming when we're both fifty. We must stop it; it's only a habit, a bad habit we've both got to get out of. D'you see?

JESSICA. Yes, I see.

HUGO. Then you might try.

JESSICA. Yes.

HUGO. Good. You can begin by taking that revolver back.

JESSICA. I can't.

HUGO. Jessica!

JESSICA. It's yours. You've got to take it.

HUGO. I told you I've no use for it.

JESSICA. What do you want me to do with it?

HUGO. I don't care. Do as you please.

JESSICA. You aren't going to make your wife spend the rest of the day walking about with a gun in her pocket?

HUGO. Go home and put it back in my suitcase.

JESSICA. I don't want to go home; you're being beastly.

HUGO. All you had to do was not bring it here.

JESSICA. All you had to do was not forget to bring it.

HUGO. I tell you I didn't forget it.

JESSICA. No? Then you must have changed your plans.

HUGO. No, I haven't.

JESSICA. Yes, or no, do you mean to . . .

HUGO. Sh! Yes, yes, yes! But not today.

JESSICA. Oh, Hugo, my darling Hugo, why not today? I'm so bored. I've read all the books you gave me, and I don't want to spend the whole day lying in bed, like an odalisque. I'll get too fat. What are you waiting for?

HUGO. It's impossible to talk to you. You want to play all the time.

JESSICA. You're the one who's playing. For ten days you've been putting on airs to impress me, and the man is still alive. If it's a game, it's going on too long; we only talk in whispers, for fear someone will hear, and I have to put up with all your whims, just as if you were pregnant!

HUGO. You know very well it's not a game.

JESSICA (*drily*). Then it's worse; I hate people who don't do what they've decided to do. If you want me to believe you, you must get it over today.

HUGO. It's not convenient today.

JESSICA (*resuming her ordinary voice*). You see!

HUGO. Oh! You're maddening. Some people are coming to see him. There!

JESSICA. How many?

HUGO. Two.

JESSICA. Kill them as well.

HUGO. There's nothing more out of place than someone who insists on playing when other people don't want to. I don't ask you to help me, oh, no! All I ask is that you don't hinder me.

JESSICA. All right! All right! Do as you please, since you insist on keeping me out of your life. But take this gun. If I keep it, it'll stretch my pockets out of shape.

HUGO. If I take it, you promise you'll go away?

JESSICA. Take it first.

HUGO *takes the gun and puts it in his pocket.*

HUGO. Now go.

JESSICA. In a minute. I suppose I can take a look at the room where my husband works. (*She goes behind* HOEDERER'S *desk. Pointing.*) Who sits there? You or him?

HUGO (*unwillingly*). He does. (*Pointing to the table.*) I work over there.

JESSICA (*without listening*). Is this his writing ? (*She picks up a paper from the desk.*)

HUGO. Yes.

JESSICA (*keenly interested*). Ha! Ha! Ha!

HUGO. Put that down.

JESSICA. D'you see how his writing slopes upwards ? and that he doesn't join his letters ?

HUGO. So what ?

JESSICA. So what ? It's very important.

HUGO. To whom ?

JESSICA. For reading his character. Might as well know the man you're going to kill. Look at the space he leaves between the words! You'd say each letter is a tiny island—the words an archipelago. That must mean something.

HUGO. What ?

JESSICA. I don't know. It's maddening: his memories, the women he has known, his way of making love, all that is here and I don't know how to read it. . . . Hugo, you ought to buy a book on graphology, I feel I'm gifted that way.

HUGO. I'll buy you one if you'll go away at once.

JESSICA. That looks like a piano-stool.

HUGO. It is a piano-stool.

JESSICA (*sitting on the stool and making it whirl round*). So here he sits. He sits, smokes, talks, spins round on his little stool . . .

HUGO. Yes.

JESSICA (*taking the cork out of a decanter on the desk and sniffing*). Does he drink ?

HUGO. Like a fish.

JESSICA. While he's working ?

HUGO. Yes.

JESSICA. Isn't he ever drunk ?

HUGO. Never.

JESSICA. I hope you don't drink, even if he offers it to you. You can't carry it.

HUGO. Don't act like a sister; I know quite well I can't drink spirits, nor can I smoke. I can't stand heat either, nor damp, nor the smell of hay, nor anything.

JESSICA (*slowly*). He sits there, he talks, smokes, drinks, swings round . . .

HUGO. Yes, and I . . .

JESSICA (*pointing to the gas-ring*). What's that? Does he do his own cooking?

HUGO. Yes.

JESSICA (*bursting out laughing*). But why? I could cook for him, since I get your meals; he could come and eat with us.

HUGO. You don't cook as well as he does; besides, I think he likes it. In the morning he makes us coffee. Very good black-market coffee. . . .

JESSICA (*pointing to the coffee-pot*). In that?

HUGO. Yes.

JESSICA. Was that what you were holding when I came in?

HUGO. Yes.

JESSICA. Why did you pick it up? What were you trying to find out?

HUGO. I don't know. (*Pause.*) It looks real enough when he touches it. (*He picks it up.*) Everything he touches looks real. He pours out the coffee, I drink it, I watch him drinking, and I know that the real taste of coffee is in his mouth. (*Pause.*) It's that real taste that will disappear; real heat, real light. Nothing will be left but this. (*He stares at the coffee-pot.*)

JESSICA. How do you mean?

HUGO (*with a sweeping gesture, taking in the whole room*). All this; my lies. (*He puts the coffee-pot down.*) I am living in an artificial world. (*He becomes absorbed in his own thoughts.*)

JESSICA. Hugo!

HUGO (*starting*). Eh?

JESSICA. The smell of tobacco will fade when he is dead. (HUGO *shrugs his shoulders.*) It will disappear through the cracks in the door, and the room won't smell any more. (*Abruptly.*) Don't kill him.

HUGO. So you believe I'm going to kill him? Answer me. You do believe?

JESSICA. I don't know. Everything looks so peaceful. And besides, it smells like my home. . . . Nothing will happen! Nothing can happen; you're teasing me.

HUGO. Here he is. Get out through the window. (*He tries to drag her away.*)

JESSICA (*resisting*). I want to see what you're like when you're alone together.

HUGO (*dragging her back*). Be quick.

JESSICA (*very quickly*). At home, I used to get under the table and watch my father working for hours.

> HUGO *opens the window with his left hand.* JESSICA *breaks away from him and slips under the table.* HOEDERER *enters.*

HOEDERER. What are you doing there?

JESSICA. Hiding.

HOEDERER. What for?

JESSICA. To see what you're like when I'm not here.

HOEDERER. Well, now you know. (*To* HUGO.) Who let her in?

HUGO. I don't know.

HOEDERER. She's your wife; keep her in better control.

JESSICA. Poor little honey-bee, he thinks you're my husband.

HOEDERER. Isn't he?

JESSICA. He's my baby brother.

HOEDERER (*to* HUGO). She doesn't respect you much.

HUGO. No.

HOEDERER. When you belong to the Party, you should marry inside the Party.

JESSICA. Why?

HOEDERER. It's easier.

JESSICA. How do you know I don't belong to the Party?

HOEDERER. It's obvious. (*He looks at her.*) You don't know how to do anything, except make love. . . .

JESSICA. Not even that. (*Pointing to* HUGO.) Do you think I'm bad for him?

HOEDERER. Did you come here to ask me that?

JESSICA. Why not?

HOEDERER. I suppose you're his extravagance. Sons of bourgeois families always bring some part of their lost riches with them, as a keepsake. Some bring their freedom of thought, others a tie-pin. He brought his wife.

JESSICA. Yes. You don't need such luxuries.

HOEDERER. Of course not. (*They look at each other.*) Come on now, get the hell out of here. And don't stick your nose inside this room again.

JESSICA. Just as you like. I leave you to your masculine friends.

She goes out with dignity.

HOEDERER. Do you want to keep her with you?

HUGO. Of course.

HOEDERER. Then see she never comes in here again. If I have to choose between a man and a skirt, I'd choose the man; but don't make things too difficult for me.

HUGO. You don't know Jessica. (*Laughing.*)

HOEDERER. Maybe not. Just as well, perhaps. (*Pause.*) Tell her not to come here again. (*Abruptly.*) What time is it?

HUGO. Ten past four.

HOEDERER. They're late. (*He goes to the window, glances out, then turns back.*)

HUGO. Have you any letters to dictate?

HOEDERER. Not today. (*On a movement from* HUGO.) No. Stay here. Ten past four?

HUGO. Yes.

HOEDERER. If they don't come, they'll be sorry.

HUGO. Who's coming?

HOEDERER. You'll see. People from your world. (*He paces up and down.*) I don't like waiting. (*Returning to* HUGO.) If they come, the job's in the bag; but if they get cold feet at the last minute, it'll all have to be done again. And I don't believe I should have the time. How old are you?

HUGO. Twenty-one.

HOEDERER. You've got plenty of time.

HUGO. You're not so old.

HOEDERER. I'm not old, but my time's up. (*He points to the garden.*) On the other side of those walls there are people who think of nothing, night and day, but how to get rid of me. And because I can't be on my guard all the time, sooner or later they'll get me.

HUGO. How do you know they think about it night and day?

HOEDERER. They've got one-track minds.

HUGO. Do you know them?

HOEDERER. No. Did you hear a car then?

HUGO. No. (*They listen.*) No.

HOEDERER. It'd be just the moment for one of them to jump over the wall. It'd be an opportunity for him to do some good work.

HUGO (*slowly*). Good work . . .

HOEDERER (*watching him*). You see, it'd be better for them if I couldn't receive my guests. (*He goes to the desk and pours out a drink.*) Want a drink?

HUGO. No. (*Pause.*) Are you afraid?

HOEDERER. Of what?

HUGO. Of dying.

HOEDERER. No, but I'm in a hurry. I'm always in a hurry. In the old days, I didn't mind waiting. Now I can't wait any more.

HUGO. How you must hate them.

HOEDERER. Why? In principle I don't object to political assassinations.

HUGO. Give me a drink.

HOEDERER. Really? (*He takes the decanter and pours out a drink.* HUGO *drinks without taking his eyes off* HOEDERER.) Well, what's the matter? Haven't you seen me before?

HUGO. No, I've never seen you before.

HOEDERER. As far as you're concerned I'm only a milestone, eh? That's quite natural. You're looking down on me from your future. You're saying to yourself: 'I'll spend two or three years with this old boy and when he's been knocked off, I'll go elsewhere and do something else. . . .'

HUGO. I don't know if I'll ever do anything else.

HOEDERER. In twenty years' time you'll say to your pals: 'In the old days, when I was Hoederer's secretary . . .' In twenty years' time. That's funny!

HUGO. Twenty years . . .

HOEDERER. Well?

HUGO. It's a long time.

HOEDERER. Why? Are you T.B.?

HUGO. No. Give me another drink. (HOEDERER *pours it out.*) I've always been sure I shouldn't make old bones. I'm in a hurry too.

HOEDERER. It's not the same thing.

HUGO. No. (*Pause.*) Sometimes, I'd cut off my right hand if I could be a man straight away and sometimes I feel I don't want to outgrow my youth.

HOEDERER. I don't know what that is.

HUGO. What?

HOEDERER. I never knew what it was to be young. I was a child and then I was a man.

HUGO. Yes. Mine's a bourgeois affliction. (*He laughs.*) It's quite often fatal.

HOEDERER. Do you want me to help you?

HUGO. What?

HOEDERER. You look as though you've started badly. Would you like me to help you?

HUGO (*with a start*). Not you! (*He catches himself up quickly.*) No one can help me.

HOEDERER (*going to him*). Listen to me. (*He stops short and listens.*) Here they are. (*He goes to the window.* HUGO *follows him.*) The tall one is Karsky, secretary of the Pentagon. The fat one is Prince Paul.

HUGO. The son of the Regent?

HOEDERER. Yes. (*His expression has changed, he looks indifferent, hard and sure of himself.*) You've had enough to drink. Give me your glass. (*He empties it into the garden.*) Go and sit down; listen to everything and if I nod, take notes.

> HOEDERER *closes the window and sits down at his desk. The two visitors enter, followed by* SLICK *and* GEORGES *who push them along with their machine-guns in their backs.*

KARSKY. I am Karsky.

HOEDERER (*without rising*). I know.

KARSKY. And you know who is with me?

HOEDERER. Yes.

KARSKY. Send your guards away.

HOEDERER. That's all right, boys. You can go.

> SLICK *and* GEORGES *go out.*

KARSKY (*ironically*). You're well looked after.

HOEDERER. If I hadn't taken a few precautions lately, I shouldn't have had the pleasure of seeing you.

KARSKY (*turning towards* HUGO). Who's that?

HOEDERER. My secretary. He can stay with us.

KARSKY (*going to him*). Why, it's Hugo Barine. (HUGO *does not reply.*) You're working with these people.

HUGO. Yes.

KARSKY. I met your father last week. Are you still interested in hearing how he is?

HUGO. No.

KARSKY. It's very likely you will be responsible for his death.

HUGO. It's pretty certain he's responsible for my life. We're quits.

KARSKY (*without raising his voice*). You're a little blackguard.

HUGO. Tell me . . .

HOEDERER. Shut up. (*To* KARSKY.) I don't suppose you came here to insult my secretary? Won't you sit down? (*They sit down.*) Brandy?

KARSKY. No, thank you.

PRINCE. I'll join you with pleasure.

> HOEDERER *pours out the drinks.* HUGO *takes his glass to the* PRINCE.

KARSKY. So this is the famous Hoederer. (*He looks at him.*) Yesterday your men fired on ours again.

HOEDERER. Why?

KARSKY. We had an arms dump in a garage and your chaps wanted to take it; as simple as that.

HOEDERER. Did they get the stuff?

KARSKY. Yes.

HOEDERER. Well played.

KARSKY. Nothing to be proud of; they were ten to one.

HOEDERER. When you want to win, you should always be ten to one.

KARSKY. Don't let's continue this discussion, I feel we shall never understand each other. We don't belong to the same race.

HOEDERER. We belong to the same race, but not the same class.

PRINCE. Gentlemen, supposing we come to business.

HOEDERER. Certainly. Go ahead.

KARSKY. We've come to hear your proposals.

HOEDERER. There must be some mistake.

KARSKY. Very likely. If I hadn't thought you had a proposition to make, I certainly shouldn't have taken the trouble to come here.

HOEDERER. I've no proposition to make.

KARSKY. Very well. (*He rises.*)

PRINCE. Gentlemen, please. Sit down again, Karsky. This is a bad beginning. Can we not put a little frankness into this discussion?

KARSKY (*to the* PRINCE). Frankness? Did you see his eyes when his watch-dogs pushed us in here with their tommy-guns? These people hate us. I agreed to this interview at your insistence, but I'm convinced no good will come of it.

PRINCE. Karsky, last year you organized two attempts on my father's life and yet I agreed to meet you. We may not have much cause to love each other, but our personal feelings have no importance when it is a question of the national interest. (*Pause.*) Naturally, we don't always quite agree as to what that interest is. You, Hoederer, have made yourself the interpreter, perhaps somewhat too exclusively, of the legitimate claims of the working classes. My father and I have always been sympathetic towards those claims, but we have been forced, through the threatening attitude of Germany, to make them take a second place, because we felt our primary duty was to safeguard the independence of our country, even at the cost of unpopular measures.

HOEDERER. Meaning the declaration of war against the U.S.S.R.

PRINCE. On the other hand, Karsky and his friends, who didn't share our point of view on foreign affairs, have perhaps underestimated how necessary it was for Illythia to show herself united and strong in foreign eyes, a single people behind a single leader, and they formed an underground resistance party. That is why two such men, equally honest, equally devoted to their country, have momentarily found themselves separated by the different conceptions they have of their duty. (HOEDERER *laughs vulgarly.*) I beg your pardon?

HOEDERER. Nothing. Go on.

PRINCE. Today, these positions have happily drawn together and it seems that each of us has a wider understanding of each other's point of view. My father does not wish to continue this useless and costly war. Naturally, we are in no position to conclude a separate peace, but I can guarantee that the military operations will be carried out without an excess of zeal. For his part, Karsky feels that internal dissensions can only militate against our country and we both wish to prepare for future peace by creating national unity. Naturally, this unity cannot be acknowledged openly without rousing suspicions in Germany but it can find its place within the existing clandestine organizations.

HOEDERER. And so?

PRINCE. That's all. Karsky and I wished to bring you the good news of our agreement in principle.

HOEDERER. How does that concern me?

KARSKY. That's enough; we're wasting our time.

PRINCE (*continuing*). It goes without saying that this unity must be as wide as possible. If the Proletarian Party wishes to join us. . . .

HOEDERER. What are you offering?

KARSKY. Two seats for your Party on the Clandestine National Committee we are about to form.

HOEDERER. Two out of how many?

KARSKY. Twelve.

HOEDERER (*pretending a polite interest*). Two out of twelve?

KARSKY. The Regent will nominate four of his counsellors. Six others will be from the Pentagon. The president will be elected.

HOEDERER. Two out of twelve. (*Sneering.*)

KARSKY. The majority of the Peasant electorate belong to the Pentagon, say fifty-seven per cent of the population, plus nearly the whole of the bourgeois class. The working class represents scarcely twenty per cent of the country and you haven't got them all behind you.

HOEDERER. No. Go on?

KARSKY. We'll arrange a remodelling and a fusion of our two clandestine organizations. Your men will co-operate with the arrangements of the Pentagon Party.

HOEDERER. You mean my troops will be absorbed by the Pentagon.

KARSKY. It is the best formula for reconciliation.

HOEDERER. In other words, reconciliation by annihilating one of the adversaries. After that, it's quite logical to give us merely two seats on the Central Committee. It's really two too many; those seats will be representing precisely nothing.

KARSKY. You're not obliged to accept.

PRINCE (*swiftly*). But if you accept, naturally, the government might be inclined to revoke the laws of 'thirty-nine against the Press, trade unions and the workmen's card.

HOEDERER. What a temptation! (*He strikes the table.*) Good. Well, now we know each other; let's get to work. Here are my conditions. A ruling committee reduced to six members. The Proletarian Party will hold three seats. You can dispose of the other three as you please. The clandestine organizations will remain strictly separate and will undertake no joint action except on a vote of the Central Committee. Take it or leave it.

KARSKY. Are you joking?

HOEDERER. You're not obliged to accept.

KARSKY (*to the* PRINCE). I told you, you could never deal with these people. We have two-thirds of the country, money, weapons, trained para-military formations, without counting the moral priority given us by our martyrs. And a handful of men without a farthing calmly demand the majority of seats on the Central Committee!

HOEDERER. Well? You refuse?

KARSKY. We refuse. We can do without you.

HOEDERER. All right, then get out. (KARSKY *hesitates for a moment, then goes to the door. The* PRINCE *has not moved.*)

Look at the prince, Karsky; he's cleverer than you. He's understood already.

PRINCE (*to* KARSKY, *gently*). We cannot reject these proposals without examining them.

KARSKY (*violently*). They're not proposals; they are ridiculous demands, and I refuse to discuss them. (*But he doesn't move.*)

HOEDERER. In 'forty-two the police were hunting your men and ours. You organized attacks on the Regent and we sabotaged war production. When a Pentagon member met one of our boys, one of them was always left in the gutter. Suddenly, today you want everyone to kiss and be friends. Why?

PRINCE. For the good of the country.

HOEDERER. Why isn't it the same good as it was in 'forty-two? (*Pause.*) Could it be because the Russians beat Paulus at Stalingrad and German troops are busy losing the war?

PRINCE. It is evident that the evolution of the war has created a new situation. But I do not see . . .

HOEDERER. On the contrary, I'm sure you see quite well. You want to save Illythia, I'm certain. But you want to save her as she is with her régime of social inequality and her class privileges. When it looked as though the Germans would win, your father ranged himself on their side. Today the luck has changed and he is trying to pacify the Russians. It's more difficult.

KARSKY. Hoederer, it was in fighting against Germany that so many of our people fell and I won't let you say that we have made peace with our enemies to preserve our privileges.

HOEDERER. I know, Karsky; the Pentagon is anti-German. You're on a safe wicket; the Regent gave guarantees to Hitler to prevent him invading Illythia. You were anti-Russian too, because the Russians were a long way away. 'Illythia, Illythia alone . . .' I know the song. You sang it to the nationalist bourgeoisie for two years. But the Russians are drawing nearer, in a year they will be among us, Illythia

won't be so much alone. So? You must find fresh guarantees. How lucky it would be if you could say to them: the
Pentagon worked for you and the Regent was playing a
double game. Only, you see, they don't have to believe you.
What will they do? Eh? What will they do? After all, we
did declare war on them.

PRINCE. My dear Hoederer, when the U.S.S.R. understands
that we sincerely . . .

HOEDERER. When they understand that a fascist dictator and
a Conservative party have rushed to help them in their
victory 'sincerely,' I don't think they'll be very grateful.
(*Pause.*) Only one party has kept the confidence of the
U.S.S.R., only one party has remained in contact with her
throughout the war, only one party can send envoys through
the lines, only one party can guarantee your little combine;
ours. When the Russians get here, they'll see through our
eyes. (*Pause.*) You see; you'll have to do as we say.

KARSKY. I should have refused to come.

PRINCE. Karsky!

KARSKY. I should have known you would reply to our honest
proposals with threats of blackmail.

HOEDERER. Go ahead. Squeal. I don't mind. Squeal like a
stuck pig. But remember this; when the Red Army reaches
our frontiers, we shall take over the power together, you and
we, if we have worked together; but if we don't come to an
understanding, at the end of the war, my party will govern
alone. Now you must choose.

KARSKY. I . . .

PRINCE (*to* KARSKY). Violence won't help. We must take a
realistic view of the situation.

KARSKY (*to the* PRINCE). You're a coward; you've drawn me
into a trap to save your own head.

HOEDERER. What trap? Leave us if you wish. I don't need
you to come to an understanding with the Prince.

KARSKY (*to the* PRINCE). You're not going to . . .

PRINCE. What's the matter? If you don't like the coalition, we don't force you to join, but my decision doesn't depend on yours.

HOEDERER. It goes without saying that the alliance of our Party with the Regent's government will put the Pentagon in an awkward situation during the last months of the war; it goes without saying, too, that we should set about its complete liquidation when the Germans are beaten. But since you want to keep your hands clean . . .

KARSKY. For three years we've fought for the independence of our country. Thousands of our young men have died for our cause. We have earned the admiration of the world, all so that the German party can join the Russian party and cut our throats on a dark night.

HOEDERER. Don't sentimentalize, Karsky; you have lost because you had to lose. 'Illythia, Illythia alone . . .' It's a slogan that can't do much to protect a small country surrounded by powerful neighbours. (*Pause.*) Do you accept my conditions?

KARSKY. I am not qualified to accept; I am not alone.

HOEDERER. I'm in a hurry, Karsky.

PRINCE. My dear Hoederer, we could perhaps give him time to think things over. The war isn't finished, we aren't down to our last week.

HOEDERER. I'm down to my last week. Karsky, I'm going to trust you. I always trust people, it's one of my principles. I know you ought to consult your friends, but I know you can convince them. If you give me your acceptance in principle today, I'll talk to the other comrades of my Party tomorrow.

HUGO (*rising abruptly*). Hoederer!

HOEDERER. What?

HUGO. How dare you?

HOEDERER. Shut up.

HUGO. You have no right. They are . . . oh God! they're the same people. The same who came to see my father . . . the

same dreary, futile faces . . . they've even followed me
here. You have no right. . . . They slip in everywhere, they
poison everything, they are stronger than we are. . . .

HOEDERER. Will you shut up!

HUGO. Listen to me, you two; he won't have the Party behind
him if he tries to put through this union! Don't count on
him to whitewash you, he won't have the Party behind him.

HOEDERER (*soothing the two others*). Pay no attention. It's a
purely personal reaction.

PRINCE. Yes, but he's making a great deal of noise. Couldn't
you ask your guards to take him outside?

HOEDERER. What the hell! He can go alone! (*He rises and goes
to* HUGO.)

HUGO (*retreating*). Don't touch me. (*He puts his hand in the
pocket where his gun is.*) You won't listen to me? You won't
listen to me?

*At this moment a loud explosion is heard. The windows blow
in, the frames torn from their hinges.*

HOEDERER. Down!

He seizes HUGO *by the shoulders and throws him to the
ground. The other two fall flat on the floor.* LEON, SLICK
and GEORGES *rush in.*

LEON. Are you hurt?

HOEDERER (*getting up*). No. Is anyone hurt? (*To* KARSKY, *who
has risen.*) You're bleeding.

KARSKY. It's nothing. A bit of glass.

SLICK. Hand-grenade.

HOEDERER. Grenade or bomb. But they aimed short. Search
the garden.

HUGO (*turned to the window, to himself*). Bastards! Bastards!

LEON and GEORGES *jump out of the window.*

HOEDERER (*to the* PRINCE). I was expecting something of the kind, but I'm sorry they chose this particular moment.

PRINCE. It reminds me of my father's palace. Karsky! Is this some of your work?

KARSKY. Are you crazy?

HOEDERER. They were aiming at me; it concerns no one but myself. (*To* KARSKY.) You see; it's better to take precautions. (*Looking at him.*) You're bleeding rather a lot.

JESSICA (*entering out of breath*). Is Hoederer dead?

HOEDERER. Your husband is all right. (*To* KARSKY.) Leon will take you up to my room and bandage you. Then we can go on with our conversation.

SLICK. You should all go upstairs, they might have another try. You can talk while Leon is doing his first-aid.

HOEDERER. Right. (GEORGES *and* LEON *come back through the window.*) Well?

GEORGES. Mills bomb. They threw it from the garden and then vamoosed. The wall got the worst of it.

HUGO. The bastards.

HOEDERER. Let's go upstairs. (*They go towards the door.* HUGO *makes to follow them.*) Not you.

They look at each other. Then HOEDERER *turns and goes out.*

HUGO (*between his teeth*). The bastards!

GEORGES. What?

HUGO. The ones who threw that bomb. They're bastards. (*He goes to pour out a drink.*)

SLICK. Bit rattled, eh?

HUGO. Bah!

SLICK. No need to be ashamed. Under fire for the first time. You'll get used to it.

GEORGES. You know something: in the long run, it takes your mind off things. Isn't that true, Slick?

SLICK. Makes a change, wakes you up, stretches your legs.

HUGO. I'm not rattled. I'm angry. (*He drinks.*)

JESSICA. Angry with who, honey-bee?

HUGO. The bastards who threw that bomb.

SLICK. You're too sensitive; we've got used to it.

GEORGES. It's our bread and butter; if it wasn't for them, we shouldn't be here.

HUGO. You see, everyone is quite calm, everyone is happy, everyone is smiling. He was bleeding like a pig. He wiped his face and smiled and said: 'It's nothing.' They are brave enough. They're the biggest sons of bitches in the world and they've got courage, just to stop you despising them through and through. (*Sadly.*) It's enough to send one mad. (*He drinks.*) Virtues and vices aren't evenly distributed.

JESSICA. You're not a coward, my soul.

HUGO. I'm not a coward, but I'm not brave either. Too nervous. I wish I could go to sleep and dream I was Slick. Look at him; two hundred pounds of flesh and a brain-pan the size of a nut. Like a whale. The nut, up there, sends out signals of pain and anger, but they get lost in the mass. They tickle him, that's all.

SLICK (*laughing*). Hear that?

GEORGES (*laughing*). Not bad!

HUGO *drinks.*

JESSICA. Hugo!

HUGO. Eh?

JESSICA. Don't drink any more.

HUGO. Why not? I've nothing to do. I've been relieved of my post.

JESSICA. Hoederer has given you the sack?

HUGO. Hoederer? Who's talking of Hoederer? That's the way; when you want to get something out of a chap like me, begin by trusting him. You can think what you like of Hoederer, but that man trusted me. Not everybody could say as much. (*He drinks. Then he goes up to* SLICK.) Some people send you on a confidential mission, see, you break your neck to do it and then just when you're going to bring it off, you find out they don't give a damn for you and they've had the job done by someone else.

JESSICA. Will you be quiet! You mustn't give them a recital of our private affairs.

HUGO. Private affairs? Ha! (*Derisively.*) She's wonderful!

JESSICA. He means me. For two years now he's been at me, saying I don't trust him.

HUGO. What a brain, eh? Nobody trusts me. There must be something wrong with my face. (*To* JESSICA.) Tell me you love me.

JESSICA. Not in front of them.

SLICK. Don't mind us.

HUGO. She doesn't love me. She doesn't know what love is. She's an angel. A pillar of salt.

SLICK. A pillar of salt?

HUGO. No, I mean a statue of ice. If you try and make love to her, she melts.

GEORGES. You don't say!

JESSICA. Come along, Hugo. Let's go home.

HUGO. Wait, I'm going to give Slick some advice. I'm very fond of Slick, I like him because he's so strong and he never thinks. Do you want some advice, Slick?

SLICK. If I can't stop you.

HUGO. Listen; don't marry too young.

SLICK. That's no risk.

HUGO. No, listen; don't marry too young. You understand what I mean, eh? Don't marry too young. Don't take on something you can't do. Afterwards, it gets too heavy. Everything is heavy. I don't know if you've noticed; it's not nice to be young. (*He laughs.*) Confidential mission. You tell me; where's the confidence?

GEORGE. What mission?

HUGO. Ah! I've been given a mission.

GEORGES. What mission?

HUGO. They're trying to make me talk, but they're wasting their time. I'm impenetrable. (*He looks in the mirror.*) Impenetrable! A dead-pan. Indistinguishable from the next man's. It ought to show, by God! It ought to show!

GEORGES. What?

HUGO. That I'm on a special mission.

GEORGES. Slick?

SLICK. Hmmm . . .

JESSICA (*calmly*). Don't worry; he means I'm going to have a baby. He's looking in the glass to see if he looks like the father of a family.

HUGO. Wonderful! Father of a family! That's it. That's it. Father of a family. She and I understand each other without words. Impenetrable; it ought to show . . . that I'm the father of a family. There should be something. A certain expression. A taste in the mouth. A pain in the heart. (*He drinks.*) I'm sorry about Hoederer. And why? I'll tell you, he might have helped me. (*He laughs.*) I say; they're jabbering away upstairs and Leon is washing Karsky's dirty snout. Are you all cowards? Why don't you shoot me?

SLICK (*to* JESSICA). Your little man shouldn't drink.

GEORGES. It doesn't suit him.

HUGO. Shoot me, I tell you. It's your job. Listen; a father of a family is never a real father. An assassin is never altogether an assassin. They're playing, you see. While a dead man is well and truly dead. To be or not to be, eh? You see what I mean. There's nothing I can *be* except a dead man with six feet of earth over my head. I tell you it's all a game. (*He stops abruptly.*) And all this is a game too. Everything! Everything I've been saying. Maybe you thought I was in despair? Not at all; I was playing at being in despair. Can we ever stop playing?

JESSICA. Are you coming with me?

HUGO. Wait. No. I don't know . . .

JESSICA (*filling his glass.*) All right, then, drink.

HUGO. Okay. (*He drinks.*)

SLICK. Not clever of you to make him drink.

JESSICA. We'll get it over quicker that way. There's nothing to do but wait.

HUGO *empties the glass.* JESSICA *refills it.*

HUGO. What was I saying? Was I talking about assassins? Jessica and I know what that means. The truth is there's too much talking going on in here. (*He strikes his forehead.*) I only want silence. (*To* SLICK.) How lovely it must be inside your head; not a sound, a nice dark night. Why are you whirling around like that? Don't laugh; I know I'm drunk. I know I'm despicable. I'll tell you something; I wouldn't like to be in my shoes. Oh, not at all. It's not a good place to be. Stop whirling round. All you have to do is light the match. It doesn't sound much but I wouldn't want you to have to do it. The match, that's all it is. Light the match. And then everybody gets blown to hell and me with the rest. Don't have to find an alibi, nothing but silence and the dark night. Unless the dead are playing a game too. Supposing one dies and we find the dead are nothing but the living playing at being dead? We'll see. We'll see. All you've got to do is light the match. That's the psychological moment. (H*e laughs.*) Keep still, by God; or I'll have to start spinning too. (*He tries to turn round and falls into a chair.*) And there you see the benefits of a liberal education. (*His head lolls.* JESSICA *goes up to him and looks at him.*)

JESSICA. It's all over. Will you help me carry him to bed?

SLICK (*looking at her and scratching his head*). He said some pretty funny things.

JESSICA (*laughing*). You don't know him as well as I do. Pay no attention. He was talking nonsense.

SLICK *and* GEORGES *pick* HUGO *up by his feet and shoulders and*

Curtain

Scene Four

The Studio.

   HUGO *is lying on the bed, fully dressed, covered with an eiderdown. He is asleep. He moves and groans in his sleep.* JESSICA *is sitting beside him, motionless. He groans again; she rises and goes into the bathroom. There is the sound of running water.* OLGA, *hidden behind the curtains of the window, draws the curtains and looks out. She makes up her mind and goes to* HUGO. *She looks at him.* HUGO *groans.* OLGA *straightens his head on the pillow.* JESSICA *returns during this and watches them. She is holding a wet compress.*

JESSICA. How charming of you! Good evening!

OLGA. Don't scream. I am . . .

JESSICA. I've no intention of screaming. Won't you sit down?

OLGA. I am Olga Lorame.

JESSICA. I know.

OLGA. Hugo has talked of me?

JESSICA. Yes.

OLGA. Is he hurt?

JESSICA. No, he's drunk. (*Going in front of* OLGA.) Excuse me.

   She lays the compress on HUGO'S *forehead.*

OLGA. Not like that. (*She rearranges the compress.*)

JESSICA. Excuse me.

OLGA. What about Hoederer?

JESSICA. Hoederer? Do please sit down. (OLGA *sits down.*) Did you throw that bomb?

OLGA. Yes.

JESSICA. No one's dead. Better luck next time. How did you get in here?

OLGA. Through the door. You left it open when you went out. You should never leave doors open.

JESSICA (*meaning* HUGO). You knew he was in the office ?

OLGA. No.

JESSICA. But you knew he might be ?

OLGA. I had to risk that.

JESSICA. With a bit of luck, you would have killed him.

OLGA. It's the best thing that could happen.

JESSICA. Really ?

OLGA. The Party isn't very fond of traitors.

JESSICA. Hugo isn't a traitor.

OLGA. So I believe. But I can't make the others agree with me. (*Pause.*) This job is taking too long; it should have been finished a week ago.

JESSICA. He has to find an opportunity.

OLGA. Opportunities are made, not found.

JESSICA. Did the Party send you ?

OLGA. The Party doesn't know I'm here.

JESSICA. I see: you popped a bomb into your hand-bag and came along to throw it at Hugo to save his reputation.

OLGA. If I'd been successful, everyone would have thought he'd blown himself up with Hoederer.

JESSICA. Yes, but he would have been dead.

OLGA. No matter what way he tries to do it, there's not much chance he'll get out of it alive.

JESSICA. You do take your friendship seriously.

OLGA. Obviously much more seriously than you take your love. (*They look at each other.*) Have you been interfering with his work ?

JESSICA. I haven't interfered with anything.

OLGA. But you haven't helped him either ?

JESSICA. Why should I help him ? Did he ask me before he joined the Party ? When he decided he had nothing better to do with his life than try and blow up a stranger, did he consult me ?

OLGA. Why should he ask your advice? What could you have said to him?

JESSICA. Nothing, obviously.

OLGA. He joined the Party; he volunteered for this mission; that should be enough for you.

JESSICA. It is not enough.

HUGO *groans*.

OLGA. He isn't well. You shouldn't have let him get drunk.

JESSICA. He'd be far worse off if your bomb had exploded in his face. (*Pause.*) What a pity he didn't marry you. He'd have stayed at home to iron your petticoats while you were busy throwing grenades all over the countryside and we'd all have been happy. (*She looks at* OLGA.) I thought you'd be tall and bony.

OLGA. With a moustache?

JESSICA. Not a moustache. A wart on the side of your nose. He always looked so important when he had been visiting you. He used to say 'We've been talking politics.'

OLGA. Naturally he never discussed them with you.

JESSICA. You don't think he married me for that. (*Pause.*) You're in love with him, aren't you?

OLGA. What's love got to do with it? You read too many novels.

JESSICA. A girl must do something with her time when she isn't interested in politics.

OLGA. Don't worry: love has no importance for women like me. We can do without it.

JESSICA. Meaning that I can't?

OLGA. Like all sentimentalists.

JESSICA. I'd rather be a sentimentalist than an intellectual.

OLGA. Poor Hugo!

JESSICA. Yes. Poor Hugo!

OLGA. Wake him up. I've got something to say to him.

JESSICA *goes to the bed and shakes* HUGO.

JESSICA. Hugo! Hugo! There's someone to see you.

HUGO. What? (*He sits up.*) Olga! Olga! So you've come. I'm so glad to see you, you must help me. (*He sits on the edge of the bed.*) Oh, God, what a head I've got! Where are we? I'm so glad you've come. Wait: something's happened. Something awful. You can't help. You can't help me now. You threw that bomb, didn't you?

OLGA. Yes.

HUGO. Why didn't you trust me?

OLGA. Hugo, in fifteen minutes a rope will be thrown over the wall and I must go. I'm in a hurry and you must listen.

HUGO. Why didn't you trust me?

OLGA. Jessica, give me that water-bottle and glass. (JESSICA *hands them over. She fills the glass and throws the water in* HUGO'S *face.*)

HUGO. Whew!

OLGA. Are you listening?

HUGO. Yes. (*He mops his face.*) What a head I've got! Give me a drink, will you? (JESSICA *pours out some water and he drinks.*) What do the boys think?

OLGA. That you're a traitor.

HUGO. They're going too far.

OLGA. You haven't a day to lose. The job must be finished by tomorrow evening.

HUGO. You shouldn't have thrown that bomb.

OLGA. Hugo, you insisted on taking on a difficult job and taking it on alone. I was the first to trust you, when there were a hundred reasons for refusing and I passed on my confidence to the others. But we're not playing at boy scouts. The Party wasn't created to give you opportunities for showing off. There's a job to do and it must be done; no matter by whom. If in twenty-four hours you haven't completed your assignment, someone will be sent to do it for you.

HUGO. If that happens, I'll resign from the Party.

OLGA. What are you talking about? Do you think you *can*

resign from the Party? We're at war, Hugo, and our friends
aren't playing games. You only leave the Party feet first.

HUGO. I'm not afraid to die.

OLGA. It means nothing to die. But to die stupidly, after mess-
ing everything up: or worse, like a fool that one liquidates
because one is afraid of his clumsiness. Is that what you
want? Was that what you wanted, the first time you came to
see me, when you looked so proud and happy? Why don't
you tell him? If you loved him at all, you couldn't want him
to be shot down like a dog.

JESSICA. You know quite well I don't understand politics.

OLGA. Well, what do you say?

HUGO. You shouldn't have thrown that bomb.

OLGA. What's your decision?

HUGO. I'll tell you tomorrow.

OLGA. Very well. Good-bye, Hugo.

HUGO. Good-bye, Olga.

JESSICA. See you again soon, madam.

OLGA. Put out the light.

JESSICA *puts out the light.* OLGA *opens the door and goes out.*

JESSICA. Shall I put the light on again?

HUGO. Wait. She may have to come back.

They wait in darkness.

JESSICA. I could open the shutters a little, to see.

HUGO. No. (*Pause.*)

JESSICA. Are you very unhappy? (HUGO *does not reply.*) Tell
me, while it's still dark.

HUGO. My head's splitting, that's all. (*Pause.*) Confidence can't
be very important, when it won't outlast a week of waiting.

JESSICA. Not very important, no.

HUGO. How do you expect to live, if no one trusts you?

JESSICA. No one has ever trusted me, you less than the others.
I've managed to get along.

HUGO. She was the only one who believed in me a little.

JESSICA. Hugo . . .

HUGO. The only one—I know that. (*Pause.*) She must be all right by now. You can put the light on again. (*He switches on the light.* JESSICA *turns away abruptly.*) What's the matter?

JESSICA. I feel funny when I look at you.

HUGO. Shall I put the light out again?

JESSICA. No. (*She turns back to him.*) You, you, yourself, are going to kill a man.

HUGO. Do I know myself what I'm going to do?

JESSICA. Show me the gun.

HUGO. Why?

JESSICA. I want to see what it's like.

HUGO. You walked about with it the whole afternoon.

JESSICA. Yes, but then it was only a toy.

HUGO (*holding it out to her.*) Be careful.

JESSICA. Yes. (*She looks at it.*) It's funny.

HUGO. What's funny?

JESSICA. Now it frightens me. Take it back. (*Pause.*) You're going to kill a man. (HUGO *begins to laugh.*) Why are you laughing?

HUGO. You believe me? You've made up your mind to believe me?

JESSICA. Yes.

HUGO. You've picked a good time; no one else believes it. (*Pause.*) A week ago, it might have helped. . . .

JESSICA. It isn't my fault. I only believe what I can see. Up until this morning, I couldn't even imagine he was going to die. (*Pause.*) I came into the office just now, there was the man with the bleeding cheek and I suddenly felt you were all dead. Hoederer was dead; I saw it in his face. If you don't kill him, they'll send someone else.

HUGO. I'll do it all right. (*Pause.*) All that blood, disgusting, wasn't it?

JESSICA. Yes.

HUGO. Hoederer will bleed too.

JESSICA. Be quiet.

HUGO. He'll be lying on the floor in a silly attitude and his clothes will be covered with blood.

JESSICA (*slowly and softly*). Be quiet, I tell you.

HUGO. She threw a bomb against the wall. Nothing to be proud of; she couldn't even see us. Anyone can kill a man if he doesn't have to see what he is doing. I was going to shoot. I was all ready. I was facing them and I was going to shoot; it was her fault I missed my moment.

JESSICA. You were really going to shoot?

HUGO. I had my hand in my pocket and my finger on the trigger.

JESSICA. And you were going to shoot! You're sure you were going to shoot?

HUGO. I was . . . I was angry. Of course I was going to shoot. Now I've got to begin all over again. (*He laughs.*) You heard her; they say I'm a traitor. It's easy for them; back there, when they decide a man must die, it's as though they scratched a name out of the telephone book. It's clean and elegant. Here, death is a job to be done. Like in a slaughterhouse. (*Pause.*) He dictates, he smokes, he talks to me about the Party, he makes plans and all I can do is think of him as a corpse. It's obscene. You've seen his eyes.

JESSICA. Yes.

HUGO. You've seen how hard and bright they are? How alive?

JESSICA. Yes.

HUGO. Maybe I shall hit him between the eyes. You aim at the stomach, you know, but the gun jerks up.

JESSICA. I like his eyes.

HUGO (*abruptly*). It's abstract.

JESSICA. What?

HUGO. A murder. I say it's abstract. You pull the trigger, and after that you don't understand anything that happens.

(*Pause.*) If only you could fire without looking. (*Pause.*) I wonder why I'm telling you all this.

JESSICA. I wonder.

HUGO. I'm sorry. (*Pause.*) If I were on that bed, dying, you wouldn't leave me, would you?

JESSICA. No.

HUGO. It's the same thing; to kill, or to die, it's the same thing; you're just as much alone. He's lucky, he'll only die once. But for ten days, I've been killing him over and over again, every minute of every day. (*Abruptly.*) What will you do, Jessica?

JESSICA. What do you mean?

HUGO. Listen; if I haven't killed him by tomorrow, I'll have to disappear, or else I'll have to go back to them. I'll say: do what you like with me. If I do kill him . . . (*he hides his face in his hands for a moment.*) What must I do? What would you do?

JESSICA. *Me?* You ask *me* what I would do?

HUGO. Who else can I ask? I've no one in the world but you.

JESSICA. That's true. No one but me. Only me. Poor Hugo. (*Pause.*) I'd go to Hoederer and I'd say to him: Look, I've been sent here to kill you, but I've changed my mind and I'd like to stay and work with you.

HUGO. Poor Jessica!

JESSICA. Couldn't you do that?

HUGO. That's what they call being a traitor.

JESSICA (*sadly*). You see! I can't tell you anything. (*Pause.*) Why couldn't you do that? Because he doesn't think as you do?

HUGO. If you like.

JESSICA. And you must always kill people who don't agree with you?

HUGO. Sometimes.

JESSICA. Why did you decide to think like Louis and Olga?

HUGO. Because they are right.

JESSICA. But Hugo, supposing you had met Hoederer last year, instead of Louis. You would think his ideas were the right ones.

HUGO. You're crazy.

JESSICA. Why?

HUGO. To hear you, one would think all opinions are equal, and you can catch them like a disease.

JESSICA. I don't think that; I . . . I don't know what I think. Hugo, he's so strong, he only has to open his mouth to make you believe he must be right. Besides, I thought he was sincere, and he was working for the good of the Party.

HUGO. I don't give a damn for what he wants or what he thinks. The only thing that matters is what he does.

JESSICA. But . . .

HUGO. Objectively, he is acting like a social traitor.

JESSICA (*without understanding*). Objectively?

HUGO. Yes.

JESSICA. Oh. (*Pause.*) Supposing he knew what you were planning to do, wouldn't he think you were a social traitor too?

HUGO. I don't know.

JESSICA. But would he think so?

HUGO. What difference does that make? Yes, probably.

JESSICA. Then who is right.

HUGO. I am.

JESSICA. How do you know?

HUGO. Politics are a science. You can prove you are right and the others are wrong.

JESSICA. Then what are you waiting for?

HUGO. It would take too long to explain.

JESSICA. We've got all night.

HUGO. It would take months and years.

JESSICA. Oh! (*She goes to the books.*) And it's all written in here.

HUGO. In a sense, yes. You have to understand it, though.

JESSICA. Oh God! (*She picks up one, opens it, looks at it fascinated and puts it down with a sigh.*) Oh God!

HUGO. Now leave me alone. Go to sleep.

JESSICA. What's the matter? What have I said?

HUGO. Nothing. Nothing. I'm in the wrong; it was crazy to ask you to help. Your advice comes from another world.

JESSICA. Whose fault is that? Why has no one ever taught me anything? Never explained anything? You heard what he said? That I was your extravagance? For nineteen years I've been living in your man's world, forbidden to touch things and you've made me believe everything was doing fine and all I had to do was to put flowers in water and bring perfume into your lives. Why have you all lied to me? Why have you left me in ignorance? Then one day you inform me that the world is cracking open, you're entirely helpless and you force me to choose between a suicide and an assassination. I won't choose; I won't let you kill yourself, I won't let you kill a man. Why lay this burden on my shoulders? I don't understand your problems and I wash my hands of them. I'm not a class oppressor, nor a social traitor, nor a revolutionary. I've done nothing, I'm completely innocent.

HUGO. I don't ask anything more of you, Jessica.

JESSICA. It's too late, Hugo; you've made me a part of your plan. Now I must choose. For you and for myself; it is my life I choose with yours and I . . . Oh, my God! I can't go on.

HUGO. I understand.

Pause. HUGO *is sitting on the bed, gazing into space.* JESSICA *sits down beside him and puts her arms round his neck.*

JESSICA. Don't say anything. Don't worry about me. I won't say a word; I won't stop you thinking. But I'll be with you. It's cold in the morning; you'll be glad to take a little warmth from me, it's all I can give you. Is your head still aching?

HUGO. Yes.

JESSICA. Lay it on my shoulder. Your forehead's burning. (*She strokes his hair*.) Poor head.

HUGO (*breaking away abruptly*). That's enough!

JESSICA (*gently*). Hugo!

HUGO. You're playing at being a mother.

JESSICA. I'm not playing. I shall never play again.

HUGO. Your body is cold and you've no warmth to give me. It isn't difficult to bend over a man, with a maternal air and stroke his hair; any child would dream of being in your place. But when I took you in my arms and asked you to be my wife, you didn't manage quite so well.

JESSICA. Don't.

HUGO. Why shouldn't I? Don't you know our love has been a farce?

JESSICA. What matters tonight isn't our love; but what you'll do tomorrow.

HUGO. It's all the same. If I had been sure . . . (*Abruptly.*) Jessica, look at me. Can you say you love me? (*He looks at her. Pause.*) You see. I won't even have had that.

JESSICA. What about you, Hugo? Do you really believe you love me? (*He doesn't reply.*) You see. (*Pause. Abruptly.*) Why not try and convince him?

HUGO. Convince who? Hoederer?

JESSICA. You say he's wrong, you should be able to prove it to him.

HUGO. You think so? He's much too cunning.

JESSICA. How can you know your ideas are right if you can't prove them? Hugo, it would be so wonderful, you'd reconcile everybody, everybody would be delighted, you'd all work together. Try, Hugo, please try. Try at least once before you kill him.

Knock at the door. HUGO *starts up and his eyes shine.*

HUGO. It's Olga; she's come back! I was sure she would come back. Put the light out and open the door.

JESSICA. You do need her, don't you?

She puts the light out and opens the door. HOEDERER *enters.* HUGO *puts the light on again when the door is shut.*

(*Recognizing* HOEDERER). Ha!

HOEDERER. Did I frighten you?

JESSICA. I'm on edge tonight. There was that bomb . . .

HOEDERER. Yes. Of course. Do you usually sit in the dark?

JESSICA. I had to. My eyes are very tired.

HOEDERER. Oh! (*Pause.*) May I sit down a moment? (*He sits in the arm-chair.*) Don't worry about me.

HUGO. Did you want to see me?

HOEDERER. No. No, no. You made me laugh just now; you were purple with rage.

HUGO. I . . .

HOEDERER. Don't apologize, I expected it. I'd even have been very worried if you hadn't protested. There are many things I must explain to you. But tomorrow. Tomorrow we'll have a proper talk. Today your work is over. Mine too. Funny sort of day, eh? Why don't you hang some pictures on the walls? It'd be less bare. There are some in the attic. Slick can bring them down.

JESSICA. What are they like?

HOEDERER. Etchings. All kinds. You can choose.

JESSICA. No thanks. I don't like etchings.

HOEDERER. Just as you like. Anything to drink here?

JESSICA. No, I'm sorry.

HOEDERER. Oh, well! What were you doing before I came in?

JESSICA. Just talking.

HOEDERER. Well, go on talking! Talk! Don't worry about me.
　　(*He fills his pipe and lights it. A very heavy pause. He smiles.*)
　　I see.

JESSICA. It's not very easy to imagine that you aren't there.

HOEDERER. You can quite well turn me out. (*To* HUGO.) You don't have to see your boss when he's got the blues. (*Pause.*)

I don't know why I came. I wasn't tired, I tried to work . . .
(*Shrugs his shoulders*.) A man can't work all the time.

JESSICA. No.

HOEDERER. This business is nearly over . . .

HUGO (*quickly*). What business?

HOEDERER. With Karsky. He's jibbing a little, but it'll go
through quicker than I thought.

HUGO (*violently*). You . . .

HOEDERER. Sh! Tomorrow! Tomorrow! (*Pause*.) When a job
like this is nearly over, you feel empty, you don't know what
to do next. Was your light on just now?

JESSICA. Yes.

HOEDERER. I stood at the window. In the dark, so as not to be
a target. Have you seen how dark and quiet the night is?
The light was showing through the cracks of your shutters.
(*Pause*.) We've been very close to death.

JESSICA. Yes.

HOEDERER (*with a little laugh*). Very close. (*Pause*.) I left my
room very quietly. Slick was asleep in the corridor. Georges
was asleep in the lounge. Leon was asleep in the hall. I
wanted to wake them and then . . . Bah! (*Pause*.) That's
all; I came here. (*To* JESSICA.) What's the matter? You
look less frightened than you did this afternoon?

JESSICA. It's because of the way you look.

HOEDERER. How do you mean?

JESSICA. I didn't think you'd ever need anyone.

HOEDERER. I don't need anyone. (*Pause*.) Slick told me you
were pregnant?

JESSICA (*quickly*). It's not true.

HUGO. Really, Jessica, if you told Slick, why not tell Hoederer?

JESSICA. I was teasing Slick.

HOEDERER (*he looks at her for a long time*). I see. (*Pause*.)
When I was a deputy in the Landstag, I lived with a man
who kept a garage. In the evenings, I used to go into their

dining-room to smoke. They had a radio, the children played on the floor. . . . (*Pause.*) Well, I must go to bed. It was a mirage.

JESSICA. What was?

HOEDERER (*with a movement*). All that. You, too. We must work, that's all we can do. Telephone the village in the morning. Get someone to come and mend the window. (*He looks at* HUGO.) You look exhausted. They told me you got drunk this afternoon? Sleep well. You don't have to start work before nine.

> *He gets up.* HUGO *takes a step.* JESSICA *throws herself between them.*

JESSICA. Hugo, do it now.

HUGO. What?

JESSICA. You promised you'd try and convince him.

HOEDERER. Convince me?

HUGO. Shut up. (*He tries to move her away. She stands in front of him.*)

JESSICA. He doesn't agree with you.

HOEDERER (*amused*). So I've noticed.

JESSICA. He wants to explain.

HOEDERER. Tomorrow! Tomorrow!

JESSICA. Tomorrow will be too late.

HOEDERER. Why?

JESSICA (*still standing in front of* HUGO). He . . . he says he doesn't want to be your secretary if you won't listen to him. Neither of you is tired, and you've the whole night . . . and . . . you've been very close to death, it should make you more tolerant.

HUGO. Leave it, I say.

JESSICA. Hugo, you promised me! (*To* HOEDERER.) He said you're a social traitor.

HOEDERER. A social traitor! Is that all?

JESSICA. Objectively. He said: objectively.

HOEDERER (*changing his tone and expression*). That's enough. All right, little man, tell me what's on your mind, as we can't stop you. I must get this straight before I go to bed. Why am I a social traitor?

HUGO. Because you have no right to drag the Party into your coalition.

HOEDERER. Why not?

HUGO. Because it's a revolutionary organization and you are trying to make it a part of the government.

HOEDERER. Revolutionary parties are formed to take power.

HUGO. To *take* it. Yes. To seize it by armed force. Not to buy it by pandering to the authorities.

HOEDERER. You're disappointed by the lack of blood? I'm sorry, but you should know we could never come to power by force. If there is a civil war, the Pentagon has all the arms and the military leaders. It will be a framework for the counter-revolutionary troops.

HUGO. Who's talking of civil war? Hoederer, I don't understand you; all you need is a little patience. You said yourself the Red Army will drive out the Regent and we shall have all the power for ourselves.

HOEDERER. And how will we manage to keep it? (*Pause.*) When the Red Army has crossed our frontiers, I promise you there'll be a bitter period to live through.

HUGO. The Red Army . . .

HOEDERER. Yes, yes, I know. I'm waiting for it, too. Just as impatiently. But you must say to yourself: all armies in time of war, whether they come as liberators or not, are the same. They live on the country. Our peasants will hate the Russians, naturally, so why should they love us, the government the Russians have forced on them? We'll probably be called the foreign party, or worse. The Pentagon will go underground again, they won't even have to change their slogans.

HUGO. The Pentagon is . . .

HOEDERER. Then there's another thing; the country is ruined;

it may even become a battlefield. No matter what government succeeds the Regent, it will have to take drastic measures which will make it very unpopular. The morning after the Red Army leaves, we would be swept away by an insurrection.

HUGO. An insurrection can be trampled out. We will establish an iron rule.

HOEDERER. An iron rule? With what? Even after the revolution, the Proletarian will be the weakest party and will stay that way for a long time. An iron rule! With a bourgeois party that will rush to sabotage all our work and a peasant population that will burn their harvest to starve us out?

HUGO. Well then? The Bolshevik Party had plenty to deal with in 1917.

HOEDERER. They weren't held in power by foreign troops. Now, listen, my boy, and try to understand; we'll take office with Karsky's liberals and the Regent's conservatives. No trouble, no arguments; a National Coalition. No one can say we've been forced into power from outside. I asked for half the seats on the Resistance Committee, but I shan't be stupid enough to ask for half the seats in the Cabinet. A minority, that's what we must be. A minority that will let the other parties take the responsibility for unpopular measures and that will earn its popularity by putting forward opposition from inside the government. They are cornered; in two years you'll see the bankruptcy of the liberal policy and the entire country will ask us to take over.

HUGO. And from then on the Party will be washed up.

HOEDERER. Washed up? Why?

HUGO. The Party has a programme; the realization of a socialist economy. We have one method; the exploitation of class warfare. You're going to use it for a policy of collaboration of class within the framework of a capitalist economy. For years you're going to lie, plot, manoeuvre, go from compromise to compromise; you'll justify to our comrades the reactionary measures taken by a government of which you form a part. No one will understand; the diehards will leave us, others will lose the political consciousness they've just acquired. We shall be contaminated, softened, disorientated; we'll become nationalists and reformers; and in the long run the bourgeois parties will only have to lift their little finger to liquidate us. Hoederer! The Party, it belongs to you, you can't forget all the labour we have given to forge it, the sacrifices we have had to demand, the discipline we have had to impose. I beg you on my knees; don't sacrifice it with your own hands.

HOEDERER. What a talker! If you don't want to run risks, you shouldn't play with politics.

HUGO. I don't want to run those risks.

HOEDERER. Fine; then how can you stay in office?

HUGO. Why take it?

HOEDERER. Are you crazy? A People's army is going to occupy the country and you'd let it leave without taking advantage of its help. It's an opportunity that will never happen again; I tell you we're not strong enough to have a revolution on our own.

HUGO. Power shouldn't be bought at that price.

HOEDERER. What do you want to do with the Party? Turn it into a racing-stable? What use is it to sharpen a knife every day and then never use it to cut anything? A Party is never anything but a means to an end. There is never more than one end; power.

HUGO. There is never more than one end; to put into practice our ideals, all our ideals and nothing but our ideals.

HOEDERER. I forgot, you've still got ideals. You'll get over it.

HUGO. Do you think I'm the only one? Wasn't it for our ideals that they died, our friends who got themselves killed by the Regent's police? Do you think we won't be betraying them, if we use the Party as a means for redeeming their assassins?

HOEDERER. I don't give a damn for the dead. They died for

the Party and the Party can decide as it likes. I'm working on a living programme, made by the living, for the living.

HUGO. And you think the living will accept your coalition?

HOEDERER. We'll make them swallow it by degrees.

HUGO. By lying to them?

HOEDERER. By lying to them sometimes.

HUGO. You . . . you look so *real*, so strong! It can't be true that you'd agree to lie to our comrades.

HOEDERER. Why? We are at war and it's not usual to give the troops a play-by-play description of the battle.

HUGO. Hoederer, I . . . I know better than you what it is to lie; at home everyone lied to himself, lied to me. I've only been able to breathe this last year, since I joined the Party. For the first time I've seen people who didn't lie to each other. Everyone could trust everyone else, the most unimportant member felt that the orders of the leaders revealed to him his deepest desire and if there was a difficult job to be done, one knew why one agreed to die. You can't . . .

HOEDERER. What are you talking about?

HUGO. About our Party.

HOEDERER. Our Party? But everyone has always lied a little. Like everyone else. What about you, Hugo, are you sure you have never lied, that you never do lie, that you aren't lying at this very moment?

HUGO. I've never lied to our comrades. I . . . What use would it be to fight for the liberation of mankind if you despised them enough to stuff their heads with lies?

HOEDERER. I lie when I must and I despise no one. I didn't invent the idea of lying; it was born of a society divided into classes and each of us inherited it at our birth. We shan't abolish lies by refusing to lie ourselves; we must use every weapon that comes to hand to suppress class differences.

HUGO. Not all methods are good.

HOEDERER. All methods are good when they are effective.

HUGO. Then what right have you to condemn the Regent's

policy? He declared war on the U.S.S.R. because it was the best way of safeguarding our national independence.

HOEDERER. Do you imagine I *condemn* him? I've no time to waste. He did what any poor fool of his caste would have done in his place. We're not fighting men or a policy, but against the class which produced that policy and those men.

HUGO. And the best method you can find to carry on the fight, is to offer to share the power with them?

HOEDERER. Exactly. Today, it is the best method. (*Pause.*) How attached to your purity you are, my boy! How frightened you are of soiling your hands. All right, stay pure! Who does it help, and why did you come to us? Purity is an ideal for a fakir or a monk. You intellectuals, you bourgeois anarchists, you use it as an excuse for doing nothing. Do nothing, stay put, keep your elbows to your sides, wear kid gloves. My hands are filthy. I've dipped them up to the elbows in blood and slime. So what? Do you think you can govern and keep your spirit white?

HUGO. One day you'll all see I'm not afraid of blood.

HOEDERER. Nice red gloves—that's smart, that's elegant. It's the rest that frightens you. That's what stinks in your aristocratic little nose.

HUGO. So we're back at that; I'm an aristocrat, a bastard who's never been hungry! But I'm not alone in my opinion and that's just too bad for you.

HOEDERER. Not alone? Did you know something about my negotiations before you came here?

HUGO. N . . . no. There'd been some such idea in the air, we'd discussed it among the Party and the majority were agreed—I can swear to you they weren't aristocrats.

HOEDERER. My boy, you've got me wrong; I know them, the boys in the Party who don't agree with my policy. I can tell you they're my kind, not yours—and you'll find that out soon enough. If they disapproved of my negotiations, it was merely because they thought them inopportune; in other circumstances, they'd be the first to do the same. You make the whole thing a question of principle.

HUGO. Who's talking of principles?

HOEDERER. Aren't you making it a question of principles? All right. Then this should convince you. If we come to terms with the Regent, he'll stop the war. The Illythian troops will sit quietly and wait for the Russians to come and disarm them. If we break off the discussions, he'll know he's lost and he'll fight like a mad dog; hundreds of thousands of men will be wiped out. What do you say? (*Pause.*) Well? What do you say? Can you wipe out a hundred thousand men with a stroke of the pen?

HUGO (*painfully*). You can't fight a revolution by throwing flowers. If they must die . . .

HOEDERER. Well?

HUGO. Well then, they must.

HOEDERER. You see! You see! You don't love your fellow men, Hugo. You only love your principles.

HUGO. My fellow men? Why should I love them? Do they love me?

HOEDERER. Then why did you come to us? If you don't love your fellow men, you can't fight for them.

HUGO. I joined the Party because its cause was just and I will only leave it when it has ceased to be so. As for my fellow men, it isn't what they *are* that interests me, but what they may become.

HOEDERER. And I love them for what they are. With all their squalors and all their vices. I love their voices and their warm hands, their worried looks and their desperate struggle against death and unhappiness. For me, a man more or less in the world, that's important. His life is precious. I know you, my boy, you're a destroyer. You hate men because you hate yourself; your purity is the purity of death and the revolution you dream of isn't ours; you don't want to change the world, you want to blow it apart.

HUGO (*who has risen*). Hoederer!

HOEDERER. You can't help it; you're all alike. An intellectual is never a true revolutionary; he's only just good enough to be an assassin.

HUGO. An assassin. Yes!

JESSICA. Hugo!

> She throws herself between them. A key turns in the lock. The door opens. GEORGES and SLICK enter.

GEORGES. There you are. We've been looking everywhere.

HUGO. Who gave you my key?

SLICK. We've got keys to all the doors! Why not? We're his bodyguard!

GEORGES (*to* HOEDERER). You scared us stiff! Slick woke up: not a sigh of Hoederer. You might give us a shout when you go out after fresh air.

HOEDERER. You were asleep. . . .

SLICK (*amazed*). So what? Since when do you leave us to sleep when you feel like waking us up?

HOEDERER (*laughing*). I wonder what got into me? (*Pause.*) I'll go back with you. See you tomorrow, Hugo. Nine o'clock. We'll talk about this again. (HUGO *does not reply*.) Good night, Jessica.

JESSICA. Good night, Hoederer. (*They go out. A long pause.*) Well?

HUGO. Well? You were there—you heard him.

JESSICA. What do you think?

HUGO. What do you expect me to think? I told you he was as cunning as a fox.

JESSICA. Hugo! He was right.

HUGO. My poor darling, what do you know about it?

JESSICA. What do you know? He made you look pretty small.

HUGO. Where I'm concerned, it's easy for him. I wish he had been up against Louis; he wouldn't have got off so easily.

JESSICA. Maybe he'd have made short work of Louis too.

HUGO. What ? Louis ? You don't know him. He's never wrong.

JESSICA. Why not ?

HUGO. Because. Because he's Louis.

JESSICA. Hugo! You're talking against yourself. I watched you while you were arguing with Hoederer; he convinced you.

HUGO. He didn't convince me at all. No one will ever convince me we ought to lie to our comrades. But if he had convinced me, it would just be another reason for killing him, because that would prove he could convince others. Tomorrow morning, I'll make an end.

Curtain

Scene Five

HOEDERER'S *office.*

The two french windows, which were blown out, have been placed against the wall. The glass debris has been swept away. The window has been covered with a hanging, fixed with drawing-pins, which falls to the ground.

At the beginning of the scene, HOEDERER *is standing in front of the gas-ring making coffee and smoking his pipe. There is a knock and* SLICK *puts his head round the door.*

SLICK. The girl's here. She wants to see you.

HOEDERER. No.

SLICK. She says it's important.

HOEDERER. Okay. Let her in. (JESSICA *enters,* SLICK *disappears.*) Well? (*She is silent.*) Come here. (*She is standing in front of the door with her hair hanging over her face. He goes to her.*) I suppose you really have got something to say to me? (*She nods.*) Well, say it and then get out.

JESSICA. You're always in such a hurry. . . .

HOEDERER. I work.

JESSICA. You're not working; you're making coffee. May I have some?

HOEDERER. Yes. (*Pause.*) Well?

JESSICA. Give me time. It's so hard to talk to you. You're waiting for Hugo and he hasn't even started to shave.

HOEDERER. All right. You've got five minutes to get your breath. Here's your coffee.

JESSICA. Talk to me.

HOEDERER. What?

JESSICA. While I get my breath. Talk to me.

HOEDERER. I've nothing to say to you. I don't know how to talk to women.

JESSICA. Yes, you do.

HOEDERER. Ah ? (*Pause.*)

JESSICA. Last night . . .

HOEDERER. Well ?

JESSICA. I thought you were absolutely right.

HOEDERER. I ? Oh. (*Pause.*) Thanks; you're very encouraging.

JESSICA. You're laughing at me.

HOEDERER. Yes.

JESSICA. It's—it's so simple. I mean I understood everything, and I entirely agree with you. (*Pause.*) What would they do with me, if I joined the Party ?

HOEDERER. See if they'd let you join, first.

JESSICA. But if they did, what would they do with me ?

HOEDERER. I wonder. (*Pause.*) Was that what you wanted to ask me ?

JESSICA. No.

HOEDERER. Then what is it ? Have you quarrelled with Hugo ? Do you want to leave ?

JESSICA. No. Would you be sorry if I went ?

HOEDERER. I'd be delighted. I could get on with my work.

JESSICA. You don't really mean that.

HOEDERER. No ?

JESSICA. No. (*Pause.*) When you came in last night, you looked so alone.

HOEDERER. So what ?

JESSICA. That's very wonderful, a man alone.

HOEDERER. So wonderful that straight away you want to keep him company. And so he isn't alone any more. It's a funny world.

JESSICA. Oh, you could still be alone with me. I'm no trouble.

HOEDERER. With you ?

JESSICA. A figure of speech. (*Pause.*) Have you been married ?

HOEDERER. Yes.

JESSICA. Was your wife a member of the Party?

HOEDERER. No.

JESSICA. You said a man should always marry a Party member.

HOEDERER. Exactly.

JESSICA. Was she pretty?

HOEDERER. That depended on the day and what you'd call pretty.

JESSICA. What about me? Do you think I'm pretty?

HOEDERER. Are you pulling my leg?

JESSICA (*laughing*). Yes.

HOEDERER. You've had your five minutes. Tell me what you want, or get out.

JESSICA. You won't hurt him, will you?

HOEDERER. Who?

JESSICA. Hugo. You like him, don't you?

HOEDERER. Cut out the sentiment! He wants to kill me, eh? Isn't that it?

JESSICA. Don't hurt him.

HOEDERER. No, I won't hurt him.

JESSICA. You . . . you knew?

HOEDERER. Since yesterday. How's he going to try?

JESSICA. What?

HOEDERER. What's he got? Grenade, revolver, assault knife? Sabre, poison?

JESSICA. Revolver.

HOEDERER. I'd rather have that.

JESSICA. When he comes this morning, he'll bring his gun.

HOEDERER. Good. Good, good. Why are you giving him away? Are you angry with him?

JESSICA. No. But . . .

HOEDERER. Well?

JESSICA. He asked me to help him.

HOEDERER. And this is how you set about it? You amaze me.

JESSICA. He doesn't want to kill you. Not in the least. He likes you much too much. But he's had his orders. He doesn't say

so, but I'm sure he'd be delighted, really and truly delighted, if he were stopped from carrying them out.

HOEDERER. We'll see.

JESSICA. What are you going to do?

HOEDERER. I don't know.

JESSICA. Make Slick disarm him very gently. He's only got one
revolver. If you take it away, it's all over.

HOEDERER. No. It would humiliate him. You shouldn't humiliate people. I'll talk to him.

JESSICA. You'll let him in with a gun in his pocket?

HOEDERER. Why not? I'd like to change his mind for him.
There'd be a dangerous five minutes, not more. If he doesn't
make his attempt this morning, he'll never do it.

JESSICA. I don't want him to kill you.

HOEDERER. Would it worry you if I got myself killed?

JESSICA. I'd be delighted.

Knock at the door.

SLICK. It's Hugo.

HOEDERER. In a minute. (SLICK *shuts the door.*) Off you go—
go through the window.

JESSICA. I don't want to leave you.

HOEDERER. If you stay, he'll certainly shoot. Come along, out!
(*She goes out through the window, the curtain falling into place
behind her.*) Bring him in. (HUGO *enters.* HOEDERER *goes to
the door and walks with* HUGO *to his table. He will stay close
beside him, watching his movements, as he talks to him, ready to
catch his wrist if* HUGO *reaches for his gun.*) Well? Did you
sleep well?

HUGO. No.

HOEDERER. You're still determined?

HUGO (*surprised*). Determined?

HOEDERER. You told me last night you'd leave me if you
couldn't make me change my mind.

HUGO. I'm quite sure.

HOEDERER. Good. All right, we'll go into that later. In the meantime, let's do some work. Sit down. (HUGO *sits down.*) Where were we ?

HUGO (*reading his notes*). 'According to the figures of the latest survey, the number of agricultural workers has fallen from eight million seven hundred and seventy-one thousand in 1906 to . . .'

HOEDERER. By the way, did you know that bomb was thrown by a woman ?

HUGO. A woman ?

HOEDERER. Slick found her footprints in a flower-bed. D'you know her ?

HUGO. How should I ? (*Pause.*)

HOEDERER. Funny, wasn't it ?

HUGO. Very.

HOEDERER. You don't look very amused. What's the matter ?

HUGO. I'm not well.

HOEDERER. Do you want to take the morning off ?

HUGO. No, let's get on.

HOEDERER. Start that sentence again.

HUGO *goes back to his notes and begins to read.*

HUGO. 'According to the figures of the latest survey . . .'

HOEDERER *begins to laugh.* HUGO *looks up abruptly.*

HOEDERER. D'you know why she missed us ? I'll bet she threw her bomb with her eyes shut.

HUGO. Why ?

HOEDERER. Because of the noise. Women close their eyes so as not to hear; explain that how you can. They're all afraid of the noise, those little mice, if not, they'd make remarkable killers. They are simple-minded, you know: they accept ready-made ideas and believe in them like in the Good Lord. We find it much less simple to shoot a man for a matter of principle, because we're the ones who have the ideas and we know the form; we're never altogether sure we're right. Are you sure you're right?

HUGO. Sure.

HOEDERER. Anyway, you'd never make a killer. It's a question of vocation.

HUGO. Anyone could kill if the Party ordered him to.

HOEDERER. If the Party ordered you to dance a tight-rope, d'you think you could do it? A man has to be a born killer. You think too much; you'd never be able to kill a man.

HUGO. I could if I had made up my mind.

HOEDERER. You could shoot me coldly, between my two eyes, because I don't think as you do about a political question?

HUGO. Yes, if I had made up my mind, or if the Party had ordered me to.

HOEDERER. You amaze me. (HUGO *makes a move to put his hand in his pocket, but* HOEDERER *seizes it and quickly places it on the table.*) Supposing that hand held a gun and this finger were resting on the trigger . . .

HUGO. Let me go.

HOEDERER (*without doing so*). Suppose I were standing in front of you, exactly as I am now and you were aiming at me . . .

HUGO. Let go and get on with this article.

HOEDERER. You are looking at me and just as you're about to fire, supposing you think: 'What if he were right all the time?' See what I mean?

HUGO. I shouldn't think. I wouldn't think of anything except that I had to fire.

HOEDERER. You would; an intellectual's always got to think. Even before you pulled the trigger, you'd have seen all the possible consequences of your act; the work of a lifetime in ruins, a whole policy blown to pieces, no one to replace me, the Party possibly condemned never to come to power. . . .

HUGO. I tell you I wouldn't think!

HOEDERER. You couldn't stop yourself. And it would be just

as well. The way you're made, if you didn't think before, the rest of your life wouldn't be time enough to think about it afterwards. (*Pause.*) Why on earth do you all want to play at being killers? They are bastards without imagination; they don't care if they do put someone to death, they have no idea what life is. I prefer men who are afraid of the death of others; it's a proof they know how to live.

HUGO. I'm not fit to live. I don't know what life is and I don't want to know. I'm out of place here and I'm in everybody's way. No one loves me, no one trusts me.

HOEDERER. I trust you.

HUGO. You?

HOEDERER. Sure. You're only a kid who's finding it difficult to grow up, but you'll make a very acceptable man, if someone helps you over the rough patches. If I escape their bombs and their grenades, I'll keep you with me and I'll help you.

HUGO. Why did you have to say that? Why say that to me today?

HOEDERER (*letting him go*). Merely to show you, you can't knock off a man who has his wits about him unless you're a specialist.

HUGO. If I'd made up my mind, I ought to be able to do it. (*As if to himself, with a kind of despair.*) I *should* be able to do it.

HOEDERER. You could kill me while I was looking at you?

They stare at each other. HOEDERER *moves away from the table and takes a step back.*

HOEDERER. Real killers don't even know what goes on in their heads. But you, you know; could you bear to know what was going on in mine if I saw you aiming at me? (*Pause.*) (*He takes another step back.*) Would you like some coffee? (HUGO *does not reply.*) It's ready. I'll give you some.

He turns his back on HUGO *and pours coffee into a cup.* HUGO *rises and puts his hand in the pocket which holds the gun. One can see him struggling with himself. After a moment,* HOEDERER *turns round and calmly comes back to* HUGO *carrying the cup. He holds it out.*

HOEDERER. Here. (HUGO *takes the cup.*) You'd better give me your gun. Come, hand it over. You saw I gave you your chance and you didn't take it. (*He puts his hand into* HUGO'S *pocket and brings out the revolver.*) It's only a toy. (*He goes to his desk and throws the revolver down.*)

HUGO. I hate you!

HOEDERER *comes back to him.*

HOEDERER. No, you don't. Why should you hate me?

HUGO. You think I'm a coward.

HOEDERER. Why? You don't know how to kill, but that's no reason why you shouldn't know how to die. On the contrary.

HUGO. My finger was on the trigger.

HOEDERER. Yes.

HUGO. And I . . . (*gesture of helplessness.*)

HOEDERER. Yes. It's what I told you; it's harder than you think.

HUGO. I knew you turned your back on purpose. That's why . . .

HOEDERER. Oh, in any case . . .

HUGO. I'm not a traitor!

HOEDERER. Who's talking of traitors? That's a question of vocation too.

HUGO. They'll think I'm a traitor because I haven't done what they ordered me to do.

HOEDERER. Who's they? (*Pause.*) Did Louis send you? (*Silence.*) You won't talk; that's right. (*Pause.*) Listen: your fate is linked with mine. Since yesterday, I've held all the trumps and I'm going to save both our necks. Tomorrow I'll go to town and I'll talk to Louis. He's pretty tough, but so am I. With your pals, you'll get by. The hardest thing will be to get by with yourself.

HUGO. Hard? It won't take long. You've only got to give me back that gun.

HOEDERER. No.

HUGO. What the hell does it matter to you if I blow my brains out? I'm your enemy.

HOEDERER. To begin with, you're not my enemy. And to go on with, you can still be useful.

HUGO. You know quite well I'm all washed up.

HOEDERER. How you talk! You wanted to prove to yourself you could be a man of action and you chose the most difficult path; like when people want to get to heaven. It's typical of your age. You didn't bring it off; fine, so what? There's nothing to prove, you know. The revolution isn't a question of merit, but of efficiency and there is no heaven. There's nothing but work to be done, that's all. And a man must do what he is fit for; so much the better if the job is easy. The best work isn't what you find hardest to do; it's what suits your style.

HUGO. I've no talent for anything.

HOEDERER. You can write.

HUGO. Write! Words! Always words!

HOEDERER. Well, why not? You've got to win. Better be a good journalist than a bad assassin.

HUGO (*hesitating, but with a sort of confidence*). Hoederer! When you were my age . . .

HOEDERER. Well?

HUGO. What would you have done?

HOEDERER. Me? I'd have fired. But that doesn't mean it was the best thing I could have done. Besides, we're not the same kind.

HUGO. I so much want to be like you; it must be wonderful.

HOEDERER. Think so? (*With a short laugh.*) One day I'll tell you about myself.

HUGO. One day? (*Pause.*) Hoederer, I missed my chance. I know now I could never have shot you because . . .

because I care for you. But don't get me wrong; I'll never agree with you on what we discussed last night, I'll never work for you and I don't want you to protect me. Not tomorrow nor any other day.

HOEDERER. Just as you like.

HUGO. Now, I must ask your permission to go. I want to think this whole thing over.

HOEDERER. You swear you'll do nothing foolish without seeing me again?

HUGO. If you like.

HOEDEPER. All right, you can go. Go for a walk and come back as soon as you can. Don't forget, you're still my secretary. As long as you haven't knocked me off and I haven't fired you, you're working for me.

> HUGO *goes out.*

HOEDERER (*goes to the door*). Slick!

SLICK. Yeh?

HOEDERER. The kid's feeling upset. Watch him for me and if you have to, stop him blowing his brains out. But gently. And if he wants to come back here, later, don't stop him in the passage by pretending to announce him. Let him come and go as he pleases. We mustn't get him rattled. (*He shuts the door, turns back to the table with the gas-ring and pours out a cup of coffee.* JESSICA *draws aside the hanging curtain over the window and appears.*) Oh, it's you again, cyanide? Now what do you want?

JESSICA. I was sitting on the window-sill and I heard everything.

HOEDERER. So?

JESSICA. I was frightened.

HOEDERER. You could have gone away.

JESSICA. I couldn't leave you.

HOEDERER. You wouldn't have been much help.

JESSICA. I know. (*Pause.*) I could perhaps have thrown myself in front of you and stopped the bullet intended for you.

HOEDERER. Romantic soul, aren't you?

JESSICA. So are you.

HOEDERER. What?

JESSICA. You're a romantic too; so as not to humiliate him, you risked your skin.

HOEDERER. You have to risk it now and then if you want to find out what it's worth.

JESSICA. You offered to help him and he refused. You seemed to like him.

HOEDERER. So?

JESSICA. Nothing. That's all. (*They look at each other.*)

HOEDERER. Get out! (*She does not move.*) Jessica, I'm not accustomed to refuse what I am offered and I haven't touched a woman for six months. There's still time for you to go, but in five minutes it will be too late. Do you hear? (*She doesn't move.*) That boy has only you in the world and he's going to have to face the most terrible difficulties. He needs someone to give him courage.

JESSICA. You can give him that courage. Not me. We only manage to hurt each other.

HOEDERER. You are in love.

JESSICA. Not even that. We're too much alike. (*Pause.*)

HOEDERER. When did it happen?

JESSICA. What?

HOEDERER. All that. All that, in your head?

JESSICA. I don't know. Yesterday, I think, when you looked at me and you seemed so alone.

HOEDERER. If I had known . . .

JESSICA. You wouldn't have come?

HOEDERER. I . . . (*He looks at her and shrugs his shoulders. A pause.*) Good God! If you feel you need a soul-mate, Slick and Leon are there for the asking. Why choose me?

JESSICA. I don't need a soul-mate and I haven't chosen any-one. I didn't need to choose.

HOEDERER. You're driving me mad. (*Pause.*) What are you waiting for? I've no time to bother with you. Surely you don't want me to lay you down on the floor and desert you afterwards?

JESSICA. Make up your mind.

HOEDERER. You should know . . .

JESSICA. I don't know anything. I'm neither a child nor a woman. I've lived in a dream and when anyone kissed me, it made me want to laugh. Now I'm standing here before you and I feel as if I had just woken up, and the sun is shining. You are real. A real man of flesh and blood. I'm really afraid of you and I think I shall really and truly love you. Do with me as you please; no matter what happens, I shall never reproach you.

HOEDERER. You want to laugh when you're kissed? (JESSICA *is embarrassed and hangs her head.*) Eh?

JESSICA. Yes.

HOEDERER. So you must be cold?

JESSICA. That's what they say.

HOEDERER. What do you think?

JESSICA. I don't know.

HOEDERER. Let's see. (*He kisses her.*) Well?

JESSICA. I don't want to laugh.

The door opens. HUGO *enters.*

HUGO. So that was it.

HOEDERER. Hugo . . .

HUGO. Shut up. (*Pause.*) So that's why you spared me. I wondered: why didn't he have me shot or thrown out by his men? I said to myself: he can't be as mad or as generous as that. But it's all quite clear now, it was because of my wife. It's better that way.

JESSICA. Listen . . .

HUGO. Leave it, Jessica. Leave it. I'm not angry with you, and I'm not jealous either, we're not in love. But he, he very nearly caught me in his trap. 'I'll help you, I'll help you become a man.' What a fool I was! He didn't give a damn for me.

HOEDERER. Hugo, I give you my word that . . .

HUGO. Don't try to make excuses. I'm very grateful to you; this once at least you'll have given me the pleasure of seeing you at a loss. And then . . . and then . . . (*He springs to the desk, picks up the revolver and points it at* HOEDERER.) You have set me free!

JESSICA (*crying out*). Hugo!

HUGO. Look Hoederer, I'm looking you in the eyes. I'm aiming at you, my hand isn't shaking and I don't give a damn for what you're thinking.

HOEDERER. Wait, my boy, wait. Don't play the fool. Not for a woman! (HUGO *fires three times.* JESSICA *begins to scream.* SLICK *and* GEORGES *enter.*) Idiot. You've spoilt everything.

SLICK. Bastard! (*He pulls out his gun.*)

HOEDERER. Don't hurt him, any of you. (*He falls into an armchair.*) He was jealous.

SLICK. What do you mean?

HOEDERER. I slept with his wife. (*Pause.*) Washed up. For a woman. (*And he dies.*)

Curtain

Epilogue

OLGA'S *room.*

We hear their voices first, through the darkness, then little by little the light returns.

OLGA. Was that true? Did you really kill him because of Jessica?

HUGO. I . . . I killed him because I opened the door. That's all I know. If I hadn't opened that door . . . There he was, holding Jessica in his arms. He had lipstick on his chin. It was all so trivial. I had been living for so long in the depths of tragedy. It was to save my tragedy that I fired.

OLGA. Then you weren't jealous?

HUGO. Jealous? Maybe. But not of Jessica.

OLGA. Answer me and answer me sincerely. What I'm going to ask you is very important. Are you proud of what you did? Can you justify it? Would you do it again if you had to?

HUGO. Did I even do it? I wasn't the one who fired, it was luck. If I had opened the door two minutes earlier or two minutes later, I wouldn't have found them in each other's arms, I wouldn't have fired. (*Pause.*) I had come to tell him I accepted his help.

OLGA. I see.

HUGO. Luck fired three shots, like in a bad detective novel. When luck comes into it, you can start on the 'if's'. *If* I had stayed a little longer under the chestnut-trees; *if* I had walked to the end of the garden, *if* I had gone back to the studio. . . . But I myself, in all that, where do I come in? It's an assassination without an assassin. (*Pause.*) Often, in prison I'd ask myself: what would Olga say if she were here? What would she want me to think?

OLGA (*drily*). And then?

HUGO. Oh, I know very well what you'd have said. You'd have said, 'Be modest, Hugo. Your reasons, your motives, we don't give a damn. We asked you to kill this man and you've killed him. It's only results that matter.' I . . . I'm not modest, Olga. I could never separate the murder from my motives.

OLGA. It's better that way.

HUGO. What? Is this really you, Olga? You who always told me . . .

OLGA. I'll explain. What time is it?

HUGO (*looking at his watch*). Twenty to twelve.

OLGA. Good. There's still time. What were you saying? That you didn't understand your action.

HUGO. I rather think I understand it too well. It was a box that all keys opened. Listen, I could just as well say, if I liked, that I had killed him in a political passion, and that the rage that came over me when I opened the door, was only the tiny momentum that helped me to carry it into execution.

OLGA (*looking at him uncertainly*). Hugo, you do believe, you do really believe you killed him for the *right* reasons?

HUGO. Olga, I can believe anything. I even ask myself sometimes if I really killed him.

OLGA. Really killed him?

HUGO. If it wasn't all a game?

OLGA. You really pulled the trigger.

HUGO. Yes. I did really move my finger. Actors on the stage can move their fingers, too. Look, watch; I move my finger, I aim at you. (*He aims at her with his right hand, the index finger crooked.*) It's the same movement. Maybe the only real thing was me. Maybe it was the bullet. Why are you smiling?

OLGA. Because you're making things much easier for me.

HUGO. I thought I was much too young; I wanted to hang a crime round my neck, like a stone. I was afraid it would be very heavy. What a fool I was. It is light, horribly light. It has no weight. Look at me. I'm older; I've spent two years in jail, I'm separated from Jessica and I shall live this odd perplexed life until the boys make up their minds to free me of it. All that is the result of my crime, eh? And yet it doesn't weigh me down. I don't even feel it. Neither round my neck, nor on my shoulders, nor in my heart. It has become my fate, you see, it will direct my life from outside, but I can neither touch it, nor see it, it doesn't belong to me. It is a fatal illness that kills painlessly. The door opened . . . I liked Hoederer, Olga. I liked him more than I have ever liked anyone in the world. I liked watching him and listening to him. I liked his hands and his face and when I was with him all the storms inside me died down. It isn't my crime that's killing me, it's his death. (*Pause.*) Well, there it is. Nothing happened. Nothing. I spent ten days in the country and two years in jail. I haven't changed, I still talk far too much. Assassins should wear a distinctive sign. A poppy in their buttonole. (*Pause.*) Well, what now?

OLGA. You can rejoin the Party.

HUGO. Good.

OLGA. At midnight, Louis and Charles were coming back to shoot you. I shan't let them in. I'll tell them you are fit for salvage.

HUGO (*he laughs*). Fit for salvage! That's funny. You say that about kitchen slops too, don't you?

OLGA. You agree?

HUGO. Why not?

OLGA. Tomorrow you'll get fresh orders.

HUGO. Okay.

OLGA. Ouf! (*She lets herself sink into a chair.*)

HUGO. What's the matter?

OLGA. I'm so glad. (*Pause.*) You talked for three hours and I was afraid all the time.

HUGO. Afraid of what?

OLGA. Of what I should have to tell them. But everything's fine. You'll come back to us and you'll do a man's work.

HUGO. You'll help me, like in the old days?

OLGA. Yes, Hugo. I'll help you.

HUGO. I'm very fond of you, Olga. You've stayed the same. So pure, so clear-cut. You were the one who taught me the meaning of purity.

OLGA. Do I look older?

HUGO. No. (*He takes her hand.*)

OLGA. I've thought of you every single day.

HUGO. Tell me, Olga.

OLGA. What?

HUGO. That parcel—it wasn't you, was it?

OLGA. What parcel?

HUGO. The chocolates.

OLGA. No. It wasn't me. But I knew they were going to send it.

HUGO. And you let them?

OLGA. Yes.

HUGO. But what did you really think?

OLGA (*showing her hair*). Look.

HUGO. What is it? White hairs?

OLGA. They came in a night. You won't leave me again. And if there are diffcult jobs, we'll get through thcm together.

HUGO (*smiling*). You remember Raskolnikov?

OLGA (*starting*). Raskolnikov?

HUGO. The pseudonym you chose for me. Oh, Olga, you didn't remember.

OLGA. Yes, I remember.

HUGO. I'll use it again.

OLGA. No.

HUGO. Why? I liked it. You said it fitted me like a glove.

OLGA. You're too well known by that name.

HUGO. Known? To whom?

OLGA (*suddenly tired*). What time is it?

HUGO. Five to twelve.

OLGA. Listen, Hugo. Don't interrupt me. I've still something to tell you. Almost nothing. You mustn't attach too much importance to it. You . . . You'll be a little surprised at first, but you'll gradually understand.

HUGO. Yes?

OLGA. I . . . I'm glad you told me about your . . . your action. If you had been proud or merely satisfied, it would have been more difficult.

HUGO. Difficult? Difficult to do what?

OLGA. To forget.

HUGO. Forget? But Olga . . .

OLGA. Hugo! You must forget. I'm not asking very much of you; you said so yourself; you don't even know what you've done or why you did it. You aren't even sure you killed Hoederer. Well, you're on the right track, all you have do is to go a little further. That's all. Forget it; it was a nightmare. Never mention it again; even to me. The man who killed Hoederer is dead. He was called Raskolnikov; he was poisoned by a box of liqueur chocolates. (*She strokes his hair.*) I'll find another name for you.

HUGO. What has happened, Olga? What have you done?

OLGA. The Party has changed its policy. (HUGO *looks at her fixedly.*) Don't look at me like that. Try to understand. When we sent you to Hoederer, communications with the U.S.S.R. had been interrupted. We had to choose our line alone. Don't look at me like that, Hugo! Don't look at me like that!

HUGO. Go on.

OLGA. Since then, contact has been re-established. Last winter the U.S.S.R. let us know that they wished us, for purely military reasons, to come to an understanding with the Regent.

HUGO. And you . . . you obeyed?

OLGA. Yes. We've set up a secret committee of six members with the government and the Pentagon.

HUGO. Six members. And you've got three seats?

OLGA. Yes. How do you know?

HUGO. Just an idea. Go on.

OLGA. Since then our troops have taken practically no part in any operations. We have probably saved a hundred thousand lives. Only the Germans immediately invaded the country.

HUGO. Quite. I suppose the Soviet Union also let you understand they didn't want to give the power to the Proletarian Party alone; that they would have trouble with the Allies if they did and besides, you'd be very quickly swept away by an insurrection?

OLGA. But . . .

HUGO. I feel as if I've heard all this before. So Hoederer . . . ?

OLGA. His attempt was premature and he wasn't the right man to carry out this policy.

HUGO. So he had to be killed; it's quite clear. But I suppose you have rehabilitated his memory?

OLGA. We had to.

HUGO. He'll have a statue at the end of the war, streets will be named after him in our towns and his name will be in all the history books. I'm very glad for his sake. And who was his assassin? A spy in the pay of Germany?

OLGA. Hugo . . .

HUGO. Answer me.

OLGA. Our comrades know you belonged to us. They never believed the story of the *crime passionnel*. So we explained to them . . . as best we could.

HUGO. You lied to them.

OLGA. Lied, no. But we . . . but we're at war, Hugo. You can't always tell the whole truth to the troops. (HUGO *bursts out laughing*.) What's the matter? Hugo! Hugo!

> HUGO *falls into an arm-chair, laughing till the tears roll down his cheeks.*

HUGO. That's what he said! That's what he said! It's farcical!

OLGA. Hugo!

HUGO. Wait, Olga, let me laugh. I haven't had a good laugh for
ten years. This is a very awkward crime; no one wants to
own it. I don't know why I did it and you don't know what
to do with it. (*He looks at her.*) You are all alike.

OLGA. Hugo, please.

HUGO. All alike. Hoederer, Louis, you, you're all the same.
You're the good kind. The toughs, the conquerors, the
leaders. I'm only the one who opened the wrong door.

OLGA. Hugo, you loved Hoederer.

HUGO. I don't believe I ever loved him so much as at this
moment.

OLGA. Then you must help us complete his work. (*He looks at
her, she recoils.*) Hugo.

HUGO (*gently*). Don't be afraid, Olga. I won't hurt you. But you
mustn't talk. Give me a minute, just one minute to get my
thoughts straight. Good. So I am fit for salvage. Fine. But
all alone, naked, without any incumbrances. All I have to do
is change my skin—and if I could lose my memory too,
that would be better still. The crime, that isn't fit for
salvage, is it? It's a mistake that couldn't matter less. We
leave it where it is, in the dustbin. As for me, I change my
name tomorrow. I call myself Julien Sorel, or Rastignac, or
Myshkin and I work hand in hand with the members of the
Pentagon.

OLGA. I'll . . .

HUGO. Be quiet, Olga. Please don't say a word. (*He thinks a
moment.*) The answer's no.

OLGA. What!

HUGO. No. I won't work with you.

OLGA. Hugo, you haven't understood. They're coming here
with guns.

HUGO. I know. They're even a bit late.

OLGA. You can't let yourself be shot like a dog. You can't want
to die for nothing. We'll trust you, Hugo. You'll see, you'll
really be our comrade, you've proved yourself. . . .

A car engine.

HUGO. Here they are.

OLGA. Hugo, it would be criminal. The Party! . . .

HUGO. No more big words, Olga. There've been too many big
words in this story and they've done a lot of harm.

The car passes.

It wasn't their car. I've time to explain. Listen: I don't know
why I killed Hoederer, but I know why I should have killed
him; because he was following a bad policy, because he lied
to his comrades and because through him the Party might
have become rotten. If I had had the courage to fire when I
was alone with him in the office, he would have died for those
reasons and I could think of myself without feeling ashamed.
I'm ashamed of myself because I killed him . . . afterwards. And now you ask me to be even more ashamed and
to decide that I killed him for nothing. Olga, what I thought
of Hoederer's politics, I still think. When I was in prison, I
believed you agreed with me, and that helped. I know now
that I'm alone in my opinion, but that won't make me change
it.

Car engine.

OLGA. This time it's them. Listen, I can't . . . take this gun,
get out through my bedroom and take your chance.

HUGO (*without taking the gun*). You've turned Hoederer into a
great man. But I loved him more than you will ever love
him. If I deny my act, he becomes an anonymous corpse, a
wreckage of the Party. (*The car stops.*) Killed by chance.
Killed for a woman.

OLGA. Get out.

HUGO. A man like Hoederer doesn't die by accident. He dies
for his ideals, for his policy, he is responsible for his own
death. If I recognize my crime before you all, if I reclaim

my name of Raskolnikov, if I agree to pay the necessary price, then he will have had the death he deserved.

Knock at the door.

OLGA. Hugo, I . . .

HUGO (*walking to the door*). I haven't killed Hoederer yet, Olga. Not yet. I'm going to kill him now and myself with him.

More knocking.

OLGA (*crying out*). Go away! Go away!

HUGO *opens the door and bows slightly.*

HUGO. Not fit for salvage.

Curtain

Methuen's Modern Plays

Jean Anouilh	*Antigone*
	Becket
	The Lark
John Arden	*Serjeant Musgrave's Dance*
	The Workhouse Donkey
	Armstrong's Last Goodnight
John Arden and	*The Business of Good Government*
Margaretta D'Arcy	*The Royal Pardon*
	The Hero Rises Up
	The Island of the Mighty
	Vandaleur's Folly
Wolfgang Bauer,	*Shakespeare the Sadist,*
Rainer Werner	
Fassbinder,	*Bremen Coffee,*
Peter Handke,	*My Foot My Tutor,*
Franz Xaver Kroetz	*Stallerhof*
Brendan Behan	*The Quare Fellow*
	The Hostage
	Richard's Cork Leg
Edward Bond	*A-A-America! & Stone*
	Saved
	Narrow Road to the Deep North
	The Pope's Wedding
	Lear
	The Sea
	Bingo
	The Fool and We Come to the River
	Theatre Poems and Songs
	The Bundle
	The Woman
	The Worlds with *The Activists Papers*
	Restoration
Bertolt Brecht	*Mother Courage and Her Children*
	The Caucasian Chalk Circle
	The Good Person of Szechwan
	The Life of Galileo
	The Threepenny Opera
	Saint Joan of the Stockyards
	The Resistible Rise of Arturo Ui
	The Mother
	Mr Puntila and His Man Matti
	The Measures Taken and other Lehrstücke
	The Days of the Commune
	The Messingkauf Dialogues
	Man Equals Man and *The Elephant Calf*
	The Rise and Fall of the City of Mahagonny and *The Seven Deadly Sins*
	Baal
	A Respectable Wedding and other one-act plays
	Drums in the Night

The Master Playwrights

Collection of plays by the best-known playwrights in value-for-money paperbacks.

John Arden
PLAYS: ONE
Serjeant Musgrave's Dance, The Workhouse Donkey, Armstrong's Last Goodnight

Brendan Behan
THE COMPLETE PLAYS
The Hostage, The Quare Fellow, Richard's Cork Leg, Moving Out, A Garden Party, The Big House

Edward Bond
PLAYS: ONE
Saved, Early Morning, The Pope's Wedding
PLAYS: TWO
Lear, The Sea, Narrow Road to the Deep North, Black Mass, Passion

Noel Coward
PLAYS: ONE
Hay Fever, The Vortex, Fallen Angles, Easy Virtue
PLAYS: TWO
Private Lives, Bitter-Sweet, The Marquise, Post-Mortem
PLAYS: THREE
Design for Living, Cavalade, Converstaion Piece *and* Hands Across the Sea, Still Life *and* Fumed Oak *from* Tonight at 8.30
PLAYS: FOUR
Blithe Spirit, This Happy Breed, Present Laughter, *and* Ways and Means, The Astonished Heart *and* 'Red Peppers' *from* Tonight at 8.30

Henrik Ibsen
Translated and introduced by Michael Meyer
PLAYS: ONE
Ghosts, The Wild Duck, The Master Builder
PLAYS: TWO
A Doll's House, An Enemy of the People, Hedda Gabler
PLAYS: THREE
Rosmersholm, Little Eyolf, The Lady from the Sea
PLAYS: FOUR
John Gabriel Borkman, The Pillars of Society, When We Dead Awaken

Joe Orton
THE COMPLETE PLAYS
Entertaining Mr Sloane, Loot, What the Butler Saw, The Ruffian on the Stair, The Erpingham Camp, Funeral Games, The Good and Faithful Servant

Harold Pinter
PLAYS: ONE
The Birthday Party, The Room, The Dumb Waiter, A Slight Ache, A Night Out
PLAYS: TWO
The Caretaker, Night School, The Dwarfs, The Collection, The Lover, five sketches
PLAYS: THREE
The Homecoming, Tea Party, The Basement, Landscape, Silence, six revue sketches
PLAYS: FOUR
Old Times, No Man's Land, Betrayal, Monologue, Family Voices

Terence Rattigan
PLAYS: ONE
French Without Tears, The Winslow Boy, The Browning Version, Harlequinade

Strindberg
THE FATHER, MISS JULIE, THE GHOST SONATA
Introduced and translated by Michael Meyer

J. M. Synge
THE COMPLETE PLAYS
In the Shadow of the Glen, Riders to the Sea, The Tinker's Wedding, The Well of the Saints, The Playboy of the Western World, Deirdre of the Sorrows

Oscar Wilde
THREE PLAYS
Lady Windemere's Fan, An Ideal Husband, The Importance of Being Earnest

Methuen's Theatre Classics

If you would like to receive, free of charge, regular information about new plays and theatre books from Eyre Methuen, please send your name and address to:

The Marketing Department (Drama)
Eyre Methuen Ltd
North Way
Andover
Hampshire SP10 5BE